ADIRONDACK Almanac

A Guide to the Natural Year

ADIRONDACK
Almanac

A Guide to the Natural Year

Tom Kalinowski

Illustrated by Sheri Amsel

North Country Books
Utica, New York

ADIRONDACK ALMANAC
A Guide to the Natural Year

Text Copyright 1999
by
Tom Kalinowski

Illustrations Copyright 1999
by
Sheri Amsel

Second Printing 2003

ISBN 0-925168-67-X

Library of Congress Cataloging-in-Publication Data

Kalinowski, Tom, 1951-
   Adirondack almanac: a guide to the natural year / Tom Kalinowski:
   illustrated by Sheri Amsel.
     p. cm.
   ISBN 0-925168-67-X (pbk.)
     1. Natural history—New York (State)—Adirondack Mountains.
   2. Seasons—New York (State)—Adirondack Mountains. I. Amsel,
   Sheri. II. Title.
   QH105.N7K25 1999
   508.747'5—dc21   99-32120
                                                                CIP

NORTH COUNTRY BOOKS, INC.
311 Turner Street
Utica, New York 13501

To Jackie
—T.K.

In memory
of my sister, Robyn
—S.A.

Table of Contents

Acknowledgments

I would like to thank the many people that have generously shared their knowledge of the natural history of the Adirondacks with me, especially wildlife biologists at the New York State Department of Environmental Conservation and the researchers at the State University of New York College of Environmental Science and Forestry, to whom I have spoken over the past two decades and who were always more than willing to answer my many questions.

I would also like to thank Catherine Moore, publisher of the *Lake Placid News,* for allowing me to practice my writing skills once a week. Additionally, I would like to thank the Saranac Lake Central School District for providing me with the opportunity to pursue and present my interests in nature to the students in the area, and Gerald Goldman for all the encouragement he has given me in expanding my knowledge in this field.

Finally, I would like to thank my family and friends for tolerating my enthusiasm for this subject and for listening to the collection of nature trivia and stories that inevitably invade almost any conversation.

Introduction

As the seasons change throughout the year, events in nature occur on a regular schedule. While some of these occurrences are influenced by the weather, and therefore can vary greatly from one year to the next, others happen on a fairly specific calendar date. These latter events are typically dictated by the length of daylight which is set by the orientation of our planet with the sun. When observing nature, it is always interesting to correlate a sighting, such as a robin in the process of building its nest, the season's first swarm of black flies, or the ripening of the midsummer crop of raspberries, with a specific time of year.

I have been observing nature in the Adirondacks for the past quarter century, ever since I began teaching field biology and ecology at Saranac Lake High School. Over this span of time I have learned a great deal about the natural history of northern New York. Some of this knowledge has been acquired by carefully listening to observations recounted by students, colleagues, neighbors, and individuals in the community who have an interest in nature. Some information has come through my own personal encounters with both the flora and fauna of the Adirondacks. Still more knowledge comes from reading everything that I have found over the years which relates to the natural history of this region.

Most nature guides, reference books, and articles in acclaimed periodicals present time frames for critical periods in the lives of wildlife in very general terms, as these sources of information are designed to cover wide geographic areas. As a rule, identical events in nature may routinely happen in the far southern reaches of New York State weeks prior to their occurrence in the northern climatic zone. One of the purposes of writing this book was to specifically cite times within a month when noteworthy events take place in the Adirondacks.

Another purpose was to bring to light a few of the many facets of the lives of this region's common creatures which are completely unnoticed by the general public. A winter landscape, for instance, although magnificent, may seem to many to be totally devoid of life. Nothing could be further from the truth. There are always events that are happening in our outdoor world. Hidden from our sight beneath the snow, in a beaver lodge, under the cover of darkness, or in the recesses of an underground burrow, life and death struggles are constantly taking place, as are more mundane activities that are of no less interest to the person with a curiosity about nature.

The following narration is my view of the Adirondacks throughout the seasons. I hope you enjoy reading it.

T. K.

Apparent Lifelessness

As you pass through a snowbound forest or meadow, there is usually little sign of wintertime wildlife activity. Tracks in the snow are few, even after a week without a fresh snowfall. One might conclude from the lack of footprints that during winter there are no animals in this northern wilderness. But much goes on beneath the snowy blanket covering the frozen forest floor and within the arching briers, dead stalks of goldenrod, milkweed, and meadows covered with dried grasses.

For the many species of small mammals that populate the Adirondacks, conditions beneath the snow are better than those on the surface. Not only is there no wind, the temperatures are also considerably warmer below the snow. At a time when a thermometer tacked to the side of a garage is reading -20° F, the temperature just under the layer of organic debris covering the soil may be as much as 40 degrees warmer.

Like most mammals in the Adirondacks, none of these creatures hibernate in winter. Mice, bog lemmings, short-tailed shrews, moles, meadow voles, and other species of voles all remain active throughout the winter months.

The most common inhabitant of forest clearings, marshy meadows, and brush-covered fields in the Adirondacks is the meadow vole. Meadow voles are rodents similar to mice in both size and general body shape, but with ears that are smaller and less conspicuous, and eyes that are smaller and more beady in appearance. Voles are also characterized by a short tail, about one-half the length of their bodies, compared to mice, which have a tail roughly the same length as their bodies.

In order to easily move through areas of dense summertime grasses and weeds the meadow vole creates narrow paths or runways. Throughout the summer, using its set of sharp incisors, it gnaws off the blades, stems, and stalks of plants directly at ground level to form numerous avenues or corridors that allow it to travel easily about its territory despite the typically dense cover of such settings.

When snow falls, matting down the dried remains of the previous season's growth, the meadow vole simply chews away any blockages that form and continues to use the runways that crisscross its territory. The corridors then become a network of tunnels on the ground through which it travels when out foraging for food.

Like the other small rodents that inhabit these settings, the meadow vole feeds mainly on the seeds of various plants, dried berries, and occasionally an insect or two. As winter progresses, such foodstuffs become scarce. Under these conditions, the vole, like its larger relatives the beaver and porcupine, gnaws on seedlings and the bark of saplings for nourishment. This girdling often results in the death of the young trees.

The meadow vole is also known to feast on the roots of herbaceous plants, especially the bulbs of various garden flowers. In places with soft soil, such as moist flower beds, this industrious rodent will tunnel just below the surface in order to get at as many roots as possible. Because of this subterranean ploy, the meadow vole is sometimes confused with the mole. The two mammals, however, are not related, and while the mole tunnels underground, it never gnaws on the roots of plants.

As it earns the wrath of gardeners, the meadow vole also menaces other small mammals that inhabit these open areas. Because of its territorial nature, it will attack and exclude other similar size animals from the area to which it lays claim. Mice, other species of voles, and bog lemmings all tend to be displaced from their homes when the meadow vole establishes itself in a particular location.

While it may force down the population of other small animals, the meadow vole is not king of the meadow. The short-tailed shrew is another small animal that sets up housekeeping in such places. This mouse-sized mammal is well known as a predator and will quickly attack and kill a meadow vole. In places where the meadow vole becomes abundant, short-tailed shrews usually follow, reducing the vole numbers. Larger predators such as foxes, coyotes, bobcats, and owls are also instrumental in helping to keep the vole population in check.

To minimize the chance of being spotted by a large meat-eater the meadow vole, and other small inhabitants of the ground, seldom come to the surface of the snow in winter. So, as you go skiing or snowshoeing, don't assume that the lack of tracks indicate the area is devoid of life, for much goes on beneath your feet.

Life Above the Surface - the Birds

For the various species of birds that reside in the Adirondacks during the winter, January is the most difficult test of their ability to survive. Prolonged periods of bitter cold and biting north winds combine to make life hard for the Adirondack avian population. A landscape covered in snow also tends to limit the supply of food at a time when the demand for nourishment is at a peak.

Unlike mammals, which usually have a body temperature below 100° F, the temperature of most birds varies between 102° and 112° F, depending on their rate of activity. For such small creatures, this high temperature is not easy to maintain during the low mercury readings so typical of this area in winter. Fortunately, the birds that are permanent residents of the Adirondacks, along with those arctic visitors that spend the winter here, are equipped with a dense covering of feathers. When they rest during spells of cold weather, or at night while on their roosts, birds quickly fluff up their plumage. This creates a thin layer of dead air between their skins and their inner layer of down which helps to reduce heat loss.

Because wind can easily disturb their feathers and draw this insulating layer of air out, breezy winter weather is especially hard on birds. During times of strong winds, they tend to retreat to the shelter found in thick conifer forests. In such areas of dense evergreens, particularly near the ground, the force of the wind is reduced. The leeward side of hills or mountains and protected ravines and valleys are also frequented during times of windy weather.

In addition to their feathers, northern species of birds gain weight from the end of summer until the end of autumn, developing a layer of fat which helps insulate them against the cold. This deposit of fat that forms just under their skin may also be used as a source of nourishment if food becomes temporarily scarce, or severe weather interrupts or restricts feeding. Ice storms in particular, which coat everything with a glaze of ice, are often the main reason birds are cut off from their natural supply of food.

The lower legs and feet of birds that winter in the north are designed to need very little heat. From the bend in the leg down there is only bone, tough tendons, and skin, none of which require very much blood. In fact, the flow of blood to the feet is so limited that the temperature of this part of their body is often only a few degrees above freezing. This allows northern birds to perch on frozen limbs, metal roofs, and wires without the threat of melting the thin coat of frost that forms on exposed surfaces during cold, crisp nights.

Another feature that helps limit loss of heat is the birds habit of resting and sleeping with their bill tucked under their feathers. When birds roost for the night, they rotate their head nearly halfway around and burrow their beak into the plumage on their back. This allows them to expel the warm air from their lungs into the pocket between their feathers and skin. Also, as they inhale, warm air from around their body is taken into their lungs and body heat is not required to raise its temperature when in the air sacs.

The shortness of the day in January also poses a hardship for birds. For most of December until early to mid-January, there are only about nine hours of daylight in which to forage for food. Additionally, many hours must be spent each night without taking in nourishment. This is far from an ideal condition for creatures that metabolize food at a rapid rate in order to maintain a high body temperature. To survive the long nights, some birds, such as the crossbills and redpolls, have a special sac in their throat, much like the crop of the grouse, which allows them to store added food for consumption during the lengthy periods of darkness.

Another important and often overlooked measure that helps birds conserve energy, and thereby body heat, is their tendency to limit movement or travel in search of food. Once they have found several reliable sources of nourishment, such as backyard feeders, birds tend to remain very close by and do not waste energy exploring the nearby surroundings for alternative feeding sites. By abruptly cutting off the supply of seeds, the birds that depend on that feeder are then forced to search for other food supplies. Such foraging activities, especially during periods of cold, blustery weather, require a tremendous expenditure of energy. This is why it is important to maintain a feeder throughout the winter once it has been set up. As long as you continue to provide them with an adequate supply of food, the birds that visit your feeder will be able to withstand the harshest weather that an Adirondack winter can offer.

Deer Begin to Yard Up

White-tailed deer may be encountered almost anywhere in the Adirondacks during the warmer months of the year. From mid-spring until the end of summer, tender, leafy vegetation suitable to the appetite of this herbivore can be had in a variety of settings, thus increasing the tendency of the whitetail to roam about its home range during times of pleasant weather.

The same is not true in the winter. Since it is not ideally adapted for withstanding the bitter cold of a northern winter, nor able to move easily through the often deep snows, deer experience greater hardships than other Adirondack wildlife. In an attempt to escape these hardships, a whitetail during early to mid-January often migrates to an area in which winter conditions are less severe, sometimes foraging as far as ten to fifteen miles away from its summer range.

An extensive lowland forest, especially one having a southern exposure, is the typical winter retreat for this popular big game animal. This setting is generally sheltered from the prevailing northwesterly winds. When blustery breezes usher in an arctic air mass, the whitetail, in a dense stand of conifers, is forced to contend only with exceptionally low temperatures, rather than the wind chill factor that can easily be twenty to thirty degrees colder.

In thick, evergreen woodlands, the amount of snow on the ground is usually much less than the amount of snow in the favored summer haunts of the whitetail. Because snow collects on the boughs of the conifers rather than reaching the ground, the snow depth tends to be substantially less in softwood areas.

Cross-country skiers may note this fact when traveling from an open hardwood forest or meadow into a dense stand of evergreens. When there are needle-laden limbs overhead, the snow never seems to be as deep. Even after a heavy wind has knocked all of the white powder from the branches, or a warm spell has caused most of the snow to slide off the needles, the accumulated snow on the ground never equals that which exists in more open areas.

Because snow is often compressed when clumps fall from the limbs overhead, the density of it in areas which deer gather in winter is greater. This better packed snow makes traveling easier for the sharp-hoofed mammal.

Deer from up to a dozen or more miles away will travel to the more favorable conditions of the conifer forests to spend most of this long season. Such wintering grounds for the white-tail are known as "deeryards," and this instinct to seek out and congregate in them at this time of the year is known as "yarding."

The high number of deer in these small settings commonly cause food shortages. After the leaves drop off the trees in autumn, deer feed principally on the buds that form on the tips and sides of deciduous twigs. Like all creatures, deer have distinct preferences for food. While some buds offer these browsing mammals a rich source of nutrients, others are seldom eaten. Therefore, not all the twigs and sticks near the ground are able to serve as a source of food.

On days when there is no wind, and when the snow is not too deep,

deer may venture out of the deeryard to forage for buds in surrounding deciduous forests. Ordinarily, snow depth of fifteen to eighteen inches in the hardwoods is enough to discourage them from trudging into places where food may be more abundant. Without the necessary four to five pounds of browse (food) that a deer requires each day to maintain its health, it begins to lose body weight and physical strength.

The concentration of deer, especially those in a weakened state, causes predators such as bobcat and coyote to be attracted to the deer yard. Thus, though the deer gains comfort in getting out of the wind, and saves energy from not having to wallow in deep snow, its chances for survival are not greatly improved after it has yarded up.

If you ski or snowshoe past a forest clearing, along the wind-swept shore of some dense marsh, or through an open deciduous forest where you had regularly caught glimpses of this beautiful creature during the summer, you now will likely not encounter a single deer sign. On the other hand, if you happen to wander into the right type of dense, lowland forest of softwoods, you may notice countless deer tracks, often forming well packed runways. If you are quiet, you may even see small herds of white-tails in the undergrowth, especially as dusk approaches. Until the snow melts and the warm breezes of spring arrive, this will be the wintertime home of these impressive wild animals.

The Porcupine Adjusts to Winter

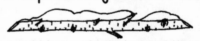

Just as deep snow and bitter cold limit the ability of a deer to travel, they also cause the porcupine to restrict its movements. As daily temperatures steadily drop during the late autumn, and accumulating snow begins to hamper the ability of this short-legged creature to move about, the porcupine spends less time roaming the forest in search of food and more time foraging closer to its den.

While this large rodent may be found in any type of woodland, it is the mature forests composed of a mixture of hemlock, sugar maple, yellow birch and beech that it prefers. Such old growth forests are quite common throughout the Adirondacks, especially in wilderness areas that have been free of logging activities for many years. In these undisturbed woodlands, the porcupine is likely to exist in any location that offers potential denning sites.

Any vacant protective enclosure may be used as a home by this plump, slow-moving animal. A crevice beneath a large boulder, a cubby under an uprooted tree, a chamber within a hollow log, or a deep hole in the ground, perhaps formerly occupied by a family of coyotes or fox, are all typical places for a porcupine's den.

Following the end of the growing season, after the summer's greenery discolors and dies, the porcupine shifts its diet away from leafy material to woody matter. The inner bark of certain trees, along with the short, flattened needles of the hemlock and a few other conifers, comprise the bulk of its wintertime diet.

As a general rule, the porcupine concentrates most of its feeding time in winter on only a dozen or two trees that are usually large and adjacent to its den. Despite its rather awkward gait on the ground, the porcupine is skilled as a climber. Upon reaching a favored hemlock or sugar maple, it will ascend the trunk a fair distance before it begins to gnaw on the bark with its set of chisel-like, orange-tinted incisors.

During periods of relatively pleasant winter weather, the porcupine may remain aloft among the branches for a stretch of several days. Its usual winter routine, however, is to feed for a couple of hours and then return to the comfort of its den, out of the winds.

Since it repeatedly visits the same trees, the porcupine develops a well-packed trail between its den and the small patch of forest that serves as its feeding area. The presence of a porcupine in an area can be noted by the fallen debris that litters the surface of the snow around its favored trees. Small chunks of outer bark, broken twigs, a collection of small sprays of hemlock needles, and a host of scattered pellet-like droppings all point to the fact that a porcupine has been, or currently is, feeding directly above.

Like white-tailed deer, the porcupine relies on microorganisms in its digestive tract to help break down the woody plant tissue that it consumes. Since these specialized microbes only act upon the inner bark of one or two types of trees, the porcupine limits its diet to those tree species. Porcupines living in different areas, however, typically develop different simple organisms to act on the main tree species in that setting. For example, a porcupine living in an area covered with beech and sugar maple would

8

develop one group of microbes, while another, residing in a place rich with yellow birch and beech, would foster the growth of other cellulose-eating organisms in its digestive system.

While these microorganisms are quite effective in making the nutrients in the inner bark of trees available to the porcupine, since woody tissue is low in protein, the health of the rodent may deteriorate regardless of the quantity of bark eaten as winter goes into its final months. It won't be until protein-enriched shoots of ground plants sprout in the spring that it begins to recover from any ill effects caused by its poorly balanced diet. It is also not until greens begin to appear that the porcupine starts to travel about in search of such edibles.

Like most Adirondack mammals, the porcupine remains active throughout the winter. Its tendency to remain within a very limited area during this season, however, means that it is only rarely seen. Trying to locate one at this time of year is a difficult task.

An Exception to the Rule - the Black Bear

It is during the spring and summer when most wild animals give birth to their young. With its harsh weather and shortages of food, winter places much stress on healthy adults; infants could never withstand its rigors. As a rule, therefore, winter is not a time for birth. Yet, for every rule there is an exception, and in this case the exception is the black bear. During the last two weeks of January, while asleep in its den, the black bear will give birth to a new generation of cubs.

Although the black bear breeds from mid-June to early July, the process of birth occurs over a much shorter span of time. After a female mates, the embryos that form within her lie dormant until very early November. Development then begins and two and a half months afterward birth occurs.

Scientists are still unsure of the conditions that trigger the process of the black bear's embryonic growth. Some believe it is related to a decrease in the amount of sunlight. Some believe that it is tied to dwindling food supplies, while still others think it may be prompted by the onset of certain physiological changes in the black bear prior to its winter dormancy. In any event, as this bruin begins its winter sleep in the late autumn, the products of its long-past mating encounter begin to form.

9

In the Adirondacks, the black bear spends the late fall, all winter, and early spring comfortably asleep in the den. Though many people have an image of this animal curled up on the floor of a cave deep in a hillside, the black bear seldom winters in such sites. A cavity under an uprooted tree, a dry spot in a pile of dense brush, or a large crevice amidst a mass of boulders are the more traditional locations for an Adirondack black bear's den. Any place that is protected from the wind, sheltered from the snow or rain, and not likely to be stumbled upon by a wandering intruder is satisfactory to the bear. Males are less selective about the site than sows are, particularly if the sow has a set of yearling cubs. A pregnant female anticipating a midwinter birth is fussy about choosing a site that is well hidden and affords the greatest possible protection from the weather.

The black bear seldom reuses its den from the previous year. New sites are checked out several weeks prior to the time for denning, and one is selected shortly before it is to retire for the winter. In the confines of its den, birth occurs very near to this third week of the new year. Considering the mammoth size of the parents, black bear cubs are exceedingly small at birth. On the average, a cub is only a half to three-quarters of a pound in weight. When born, it is blind and covered with only a fine coat of hair. In order to keep warm, the cub must nuzzle in the thick, warm fur of its mother.

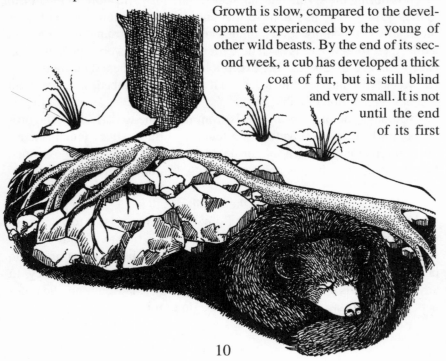

Growth is slow, compared to the development experienced by the young of other wild beasts. By the end of its second week, a cub has developed a thick coat of fur, but is still blind and very small. It is not until the end of its first month that its eyes open, though its eyesight at this stage is still extremely poor and does not improve much until the end of its second month of life. At this time, and throughout the third month, teeth form and the cub begins using its legs more.

By late April the cubs are ready to leave the safety of the den to begin the daily exploration of a landscape that is becoming more hospitable to life. The sow keeps an especially close eye on her cubs during this critical period. Although few predators would dare to attack a cub under the close supervision of a 200- to 300-pound parent, one that has strayed too far from its mother quickly becomes fair game for other carnivores with an appetite.

The cubs remain with their mother throughout the summer and autumn and will sleep with her during the next winter. When they emerge the following spring, the cubs are increasingly ignored by the sow until they are eventually abandoned as June and another mating season arrives. Unlike all other creatures which inhabit the Adirondacks, the black bear breeds only every other year.

As snow accumulates on the frozen forest floor, and winter gales howl through barren branches, there is new life entering the world. Tucked away in the protective cover of dens all across the mountain wilderness, during the third or fourth week of January black bears will be experiencing the miracle of birth.

The Beaver's Breeding Season Arrives

While mid-January brings an end to the embryonic development of the black bear, it is the time when this process is just beginning in many beavers. Starting around the third or fourth week of this month, this massive mammal with its flat, oval tail experiences an awakening mating urge.

Despite many notions to the contrary, the beaver does not hibernate. As the thickness of the ice covering its pond increases to the point at which it can no longer break through, the beaver settles into a simple routine of rest and sleep, intermixed with feeding periods.

During autumn, the beaver assembles a sizeable cache of sticks and twigs immediately outside the underwater entrance to its lodge. When it becomes hungry, it merely plunges into its exit hole, swims a few feet below the ice, and grabs one of the many branches in its submerged food reserve. A beaver will usually have to gnaw off the top of the limb in order to free it from the solid layer of ice overhead that steadily grows thicker with each successive blast of arctic air.

The greatly reduced amount of oxygen inside the lodge is the main reason a beaver's activity is limited during this season. Only very small amounts of air are able to permeate the thick mud and stick walls of the lodge, or bubble out of the water that fills the entrance. A reduced level of activity helps to decrease the rate of oxygen consumption and maintain a livable atmosphere.

While the thick wall of its lodge restricts oxygen from entering, this now frozen, snow covered barrier is extremely effective in preventing intruders and the cold from getting in. The temperature inside the living chamber seldom dips below freezing, even though the outside air may be well below zero. This is why the water that fills the entrance hole inside the lodge does not freeze.

In northern areas like the Adirondacks, one danger that confronts beavers is the possibility of becoming entrapped in the lodge. Although ice does not form over the inside entrance, it may develop at the other end. During severe winters, especially in lakes where there is no current to circulate the water, the ice outside the lodge may form well below the level of the exit tunnel. If this happens, the family will be unable to reach their food pile and eventually will die of starvation. Although their sharp incisors can gnaw through wood, they are unable to cut through a substantial ice blockage. Also, because of the cold, the mud that was packed into the walls of the lodge during the autumn is now hard like concrete. While the beavers may attempt to free themselves by chewing on the sticks inside, escape is virtually impossible.

Because of the especially thick covering of ice that forms

over bodies of water in the Adirondacks, a beaver seldom ventures beyond the boundaries of the lake, stream, or woodland pond that serves as its home. Since, as mid-winter arrives and breeding time approaches, the male is unable to travel to other areas to search for females, the single adult male in a lodge will breed only with the resident female.

The beaver is a territorial animal and there is never more than one pair of adult beavers in an area at the same time. Throughout the spring, summer, and fall the adults that occupy a particular aquatic area will periodically advertise their claim to that location with the creation of scent posts. These are small mounds of matter placed in certain spots along the waterway which are treated from time to time with a chemical from their scent glands.

While the mating urge awakens during the latter half of January, the peak of the breeding season is reported by wildlife biologists to be in the early to middle part of February. Following what is considered to be a quiet mating season relative to that of other mammals, the couple, with the young from the past two years, continue their mundane routine of resting, eating, and sleeping.

Since the gestation period is about three and a half months, beaver kits are born beginning in early May. This is the time when new vegetation is rapidly sprouting and fresh, nutritious edibles are everywhere. For now, however, the beaver must be content to nibble only on waterlogged tree bark, anticipating the coming of better food in the spring.

Inactive Insects

Winter weather in the Adirondacks can be extremely harsh, as anyone who lives in the area surely knows. Still, regardless of the severity of the season, there always seems to be one or more periods of intense thaw. While these annual spells of unseasonably mild weather benefit many creatures, the largest and most diverse group of animals that populate the Adirondacks remain totally unaffected. For insects and other invertebrates, mid-winter thaws pass without having the slightest impact.

Many northern varieties of bugs spend this season underwater in an aquatic stage of their life cycle. Black flies are perhaps the best known for this, yet mayflies, stoneflies, dragonflies, damselflies, caddisflies, and a host of other insects survive the winter embedded in the mud, tucked under a submerged tree, or covered by particles of gravel well below the covering of ice. Since the warmth of the air during a thaw is unable to elevate the temperature of the near freezing water, a mild spell has virtually no impact on the creatures that winter on the bottom of a stream or the bed of a lake. It is not until mid-spring, often several weeks to a month after the ice goes out, that the water begins to warm sufficiently to cause these invertebrates to emerge from their dormant state.

The situation is similar for the many forms of life that winter in the frozen soil. Numerous species of grasshoppers and crickets, for example, deposit their eggs during late summer or fall, either in the layer of organic debris covering the ground, or in the upper surface of the soil. Although the temperature of these eggs may drop well below 32° F, the microscopic embryos inside are able to remain alive as a result of various physiological changes. The low moisture levels in the ' cells, coupled with their high fat concentrations, prevent any water in them from freezing at the normal wintertime soil temperatures. The eggs of some species of ground dwelling bugs in the Adirondacks are even capable of withstanding temperatures near zero before ice crystals begin to form in them. Although the snow may vanish from some areas during times of mid-winter thaws, the soil typically remains frozen, or very close to

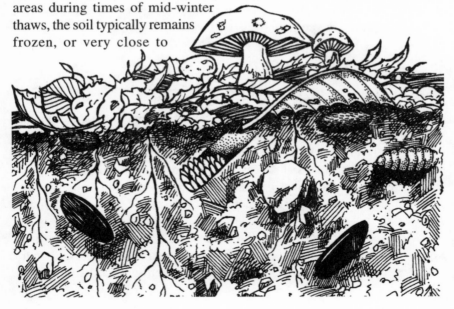

freezing, thereby preventing the premature development of these eggs.

The bugs that winter under the bark of trees are regulated by a type of hibernation known as *diapause*. These insects remain dormant throughout periods of mild weather since their state of inactivity is not regulated by surrounding temperatures. The onset of diapause is triggered by the shortened length of daylight during autumn when these bugs begin to seek out a sheltered area above the ground that is to serve as their wintering site. Although

the weather may remain mild with conditions favorable for continued activity, their urge to become dormant overpowers all else, and they sink into their torpid state.

Internal changes occur in the body of these insects to protect them from the bitter cold. In the case of a certain species of caterpillar, entomologists have noted changes that allow ice crystals in the cells to form without affecting the cell's ability to function properly. These changes are necessary for development to proceed to the next stage. Thus, if an insect is captured and brought into a warm, well lit room, its life cycle will be unable to continue, despite the abundance of food and other conditions necessary to sustain life.

A biological alarm clock in the invertebrate tells it when to emerge from this state of dormancy. Despite mild weather in winter, or an early spring, these bugs remain inactive until a predetermined time, preventing them from emerging from their hibernation too early. This could result in the insect's death, since food sources may not be available at that early date.

Not only does diapause prevent a premature awakening, it also helps to synchronize the life cycles of these insects. Certain species of bark beetles, for example, simultaneously emerge from their winter sleep. This causes all of them to be ready for their late spring breeding season at exactly the same time, which dramatically improves the chances of two receptive adults locating each other.

The January Thaw

The last week of January is the time of its traditional thaw. Unseasonably warm weather, along with an occasional rain shower, inevitably makes a mess of the skiing and causes icy ruts on the road.

For many of the wild creatures of the Adirondacks, the thaw provides a break from their winter routine. The tracks of a black bear may be seen leaving a deep depression under an uprooted tree as the males take advantage of a spell of mild weather to arise from their period of dormancy, stretch their legs, and nose about the areas they left nearly two months earlier. A sow with yearling cubs may also get up at this time; however, a female that has recently given birth will always remain in her den, regardless of how pleasant the weather may become.

The raccoon and skunk are two other winter sleepers that may seize the opportunity to quickly check on the conditions around their immediate area. It is believed that these creatures seldom eat anything during their brief mid-winter outings. Apparently, they arise only to satisfy their curiosity about the state of affairs in their wilderness neighborhood.

The chipmunk, which enters a much deeper state of inactivity in the autumn, may also be aroused by a mid-winter thaw.

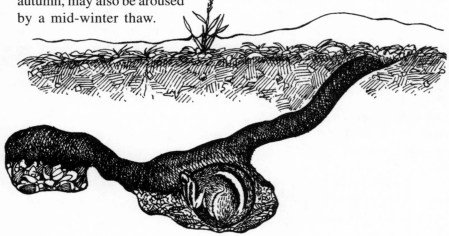

Ordinarily this striped member of the squirrel family stirs from its semi-hibernation state once every few days throughout the winter to nibble on its cache of maple seeds and beechnuts gathered the previous year. Should a chipmunk sense that the weather above has turned spring-like, it may be inclined to exit through one of its unplugged tunnel openings, perhaps simply to get a breath of fresh air. Since chipmunks do not travel well on snow, they usually spend very little time on the surface before retreating into their burrows again.

The small birds that populate the Adirondacks in winter also welcome a thaw, especially if it is free of rain. During an unseasonably mild spell, birds are able to take short breaks from their day-long battle to maintain a constant body temperature. Heavy rains, however, can mat down their feathery coat and cause a loss of heat similar to that experienced during much colder weather.

During their respites from feeding, birds usually explore their surroundings for new and untapped sources of food. Occasionally, during a thaw, you may hear a chickadee giving its springtime "Feee-be-be" call. This is the bird's mating song, and apparently there is a member of every flock that knows it is never too early to express its willingness to mate once the breeding season arrives several months from now.

Deer also take advantage of warm weather by leaving the confines of their wintering area. Since cold and blustery conditions are the primary reason that these animals are forced into the deer yards, the absence of this winter weather allows the whitetail to come out. If the snow is not too deep, deer will wander into the open hardwoods where browse is more abundant, and may remain there until the weather turns cold again.

For predators that rely on their sense of smell to locate food, such as the coyote and fox, a thaw can be a blessing. Since scent tends to linger in the air when the relative humidity is high, a period of melting usually produces ideal conditions for these animals to locate prey using their sense of smell. Warmer weather also tends to compact the snow that is on the ground. Thus, when the cold returns, the more dense snow is easier to travel across for animals such as the coyote and fox.

It is a delight for most people to wake up on a sunny morning in late January when the wood stove does not have to be stoked immediately after getting out of bed. While such weather may not be the best for the ski industry, most people, and nearly every form of wildlife, find it to be a welcome respite.

Groundhog Day in the Adirondacks

This week the attention of the nation will be focused on a large rodent that resides in a very special place in Punxsutawney, Pennsylvania. Groundhog Day is celebrated on the second day of this month. Weather prognosticators and folklore enthusiasts across the country will be interested in whether or not the groundhog sees its shadow when it briefly emerges from its burrow.

The Keystone State groundhog's ability to make long range weather forecasts isn't the only reason it is different from other groundhogs. On February 2 most of them are tightly curled up and hibernating in a grass-lined chamber well underground, rather than peeking out from their entrance.

Though it may not look like it, the groundhog, or woodchuck as it is better known in the Adirondacks, is a member of the squirrel family. It prefers to inhabit open fields and brushy meadows, especially near hardwood forests, and it ranges from central Dixie all the way up to Hudson Bay. Unlike squirrels, the woodchuck does not spend the winter under a bird feeder picking up sunflower seeds that have fallen to the ground. During autumn, this chubby-looking animal enters a deep room in its subterranean complex of tunnels and chambers to retire until spring.

Unlike the bear, raccoon, and skunk, the woodchuck enters into an especially deep state of dormancy during these months. Known as a true state of hibernation, this prolonged period of inactivity is marked by a drastic lowering of the woodchuck's overall metabolism resulting in a substantial drop in its body temperature.

The woodchuck remains in this torpid state until the ground around it sufficiently warms. Because the soil is slow to warm during mild spells in mid-winter, periods of unseasonably warm weather do not usually disturb this animal. In the extreme southern portions of its range, woodchucks have been known to awaken during February. When they do, however, they will wander for only brief periods outside their den. Once the temperature turns cold again, they will quickly return and re-enter their state of hibernation.

In the Adirondacks, cases of premature awakening are rare in late winter and unheard of during the first week of February. It is unusual, therefore, to see a woodchuck before St. Patrick's Day, and it is not until early to mid-April that they traditionally shake off their winter drowsiness and get ready for spring. Within several days to a week after emerging from their long winter sleep, the male begins to look for females with which to mate.

During the first spell of spring weather the woodchuck not only searches for a mate, but also for a different burrow that will serve as its summer residence. In winter, the groundhog lives in a burrow that is often dug into a well-sloped hillside in a heavily wooded area where the problem of flooding from spring rains and snow melt is minimal. In these areas, however, there are few tender ground plants to eat. After the danger of flooding passes, usually during mid- to late April, the woodchuck is drawn toward more level ground where the soil is richer and the vegetation more succulent and nutritious. However, in the Adirondacks, since most open areas are adjacent to adequately drained hillsides, winter and summer burrow systems are often combined into a single complex.

The woodchuck, a grazing creature, never wanders too far from a field or meadow. It is in such open settings that the tender shoots of newly sprouted grasses and the emerging leaves of dandelions, buttercups, and chickweeds grow in greatest abundance, providing the woodchuck with a choice selection of foodstuffs.

It will be enough on February 2 to just experience the joy of visiting open areas in winter on calm, sunny days without expecting to see a groundhog. If you are in need of a long range forecast, it is best to contact the National Weather Service, or listen to the news of a report on the results of Punxsutawney Phil's outing. Adirondack groundhogs are asleep on that day and will remain so until Spring.

Where Winter Weather is Worst

While winter weather can be harsh around the towns and villages of the Adirondacks, conditions become even more extreme at higher elevations, and reach their most severe intensity at the summits of the High Peaks. At the top of the tallest mountains in the Adirondacks, the weather during the winter often becomes as inhospitable to life as that which exists anywhere else on the surface of the earth. During those times when a mass of arctic air invades the region, conditions for dehydration increase greatly, as arctic air tends to be exceptionally dry. It is dehydration that leads to the death of the trees, shrubs, and ground plants that grow on the upper mountain slopes.

All living organisms require the presence of water in their tissues, and plants are no exception. Even though vegetation is currently in a dormant state, minimal levels of moisture are still needed inside their cells to maintain life. Exceedingly low humidity causes an increase in the amount of evaporation of moisture that is present in objects in the environment. Though the water may be locked inside the protective structure of living

tissues, the dryness of the air in winter is capable of drawing out this vital compound from cells. Because of this drying effect, many people place a pot of water on their wood stove, vent their clothes dryer back into their house, or activate a humidifier to prevent wooden furniture from cracking, skin from chapping, and throats from becoming scratchy. The lower temperatures at higher elevations correspond to an increased level of dryness, creating a more adverse climate for the plants that exist at these altitudes.

Wind is another element that causes moisture to be drawn into the air from exposed objects. At higher elevations the wind is always blowing harder than in the lowlands, making conditions for dehydration more severe.

Places exposed to the full fury of the prevailing winds are those where desiccation (drying out) is most pronounced. The vegetation that grows on these sites tends to develop in dense clusters and never reaches any appreciable height. The thick, shrubby nature of these tightly spaced plants allows snow and ice to accumulate in and around their surfaces. Such a protective covering helps trap in moisture while sheltering them from the wind.

At or above the timberline, winter drying conditions are so severe that the only plants capable of surviving are those that develop a covering of ice or snow. In spots where snowdrifts develop, such as downwind from a massive boulder or in a surface depression, plants usually grow as high as the accumulated snow. But along windswept ridges or on the surface of rocks that face northwest little snow gets a chance to settle. This prevents most forms of life, except for some hardy species of arctic lichens, from existing in these places that resemble the desolate land masses near the North Pole.

In more sheltered areas, or on a slope further down from the summit, a tree can only support limbs on the leeward side of its usually gnarled trunk. Should a twig or branch sprout during the summer in a direction that exposes it to the winter's gales, it would quickly succumb to the desiccating effect of the wind. Trees that have branches growing in only one direction are known as flag trees and are helpful to atmospheric scientists in determining the direction that the dry, prevailing winds blow across that site.

The severity of the climate in most locations can best be noted by the type of trees in the area. For instance, at the base of Whiteface Mountain, there are forests of hardwood trees. As you ride the chairlift up the mountain, you can see that the deciduous woodlands gradually develop into evergreen forests. This is because conifers are far better adapted for tolerating the rigors of the colder, sub-arctic climate existing at these higher elevations.

Near the top, the evergreens become dwarfed and the forests thicken until, at the summit, only scattered patches of dense small plants are present. These are covered with a frosting-like layer of ice and snow that keeps them protected from winter's dry wind and also makes for a most picturesque photograph.

The Winter Life of an Otter

Few natural settings are changed as dramatically by winter's cold as the pristine waterways of the Adirondacks. The thick layer of ice that develops over lakes, ponds, marshes, and rivers cuts off access to the air above. This causes waterfowl, loons, wading birds, and gulls to retreat to milder climates where there is open water. Ice also restricts the movement and activities of the beaver and muskrat.

For the otter, however, life continues in much the same manner as during the warmer months of the year, except that less time is spent along larger waterways. As the surface of the lakes freezes solid, the otter begins to concentrate more of its time in the tributaries that feed them.

Despite prolonged periods of bitter cold, there are always open holes in streams and rivers which allow this sleek member of the weasel family access to the water to travel fair distances beneath the transparent covering. When water cascades over rocks and swirls around boulders, it mixes with air and acquires dissolved oxygen. As the water moves downstream, some of this air is released and bubbles upward, forming small air pockets. When moving beneath the surface, an otter will frequently come up to breathe this trapped air. On occasion, it may also venture out into a lake, utilizing the air pockets that form, especially around the mouth of inflowing streams and brooks.

The dense covering of fur which makes the hide of an otter so valuable to trappers is extremely effective in helping it retain body heat while immersed in the freezing water. Layers of fat insulate it and prevent the otter from developing an acute case of hypothermia.

The rich bounty of food available in the water makes it possible for an otter to be well fed during this bleak season. Small forms of aquatic life, such as crayfish, frogs, salamanders, fresh water mussels, snails, and assorted types of fish, compose the bulk of its diet. Because these creatures are cold-blooded, they either become extremely lethargic in the near-freezing water, or enter a dormant state. With its four webbed feet and thick muscular tail, which also helps to propel it through the water, the otter is well known for being able to outswim minnows, chubs, and even brook trout in the spring and summer. Catching fish in winter poses little problem for this aquatic predator. If no fish are flushed from their hiding spots, the otter simply digs into the mud to uncover wintering animals. It usually does this standing upside-down, with its head pressed against the bottom.

The otter may use several locations to rest during the day, or retreat to during periods of inclement weather. Typical sites for dens include abandoned beaver lodges, rocky cubbies, hollow logs, or other similar types of protective enclosures, especially along the edge of a flowing body of water. In early to mid-February, the female otter begins to favor one of these sites over any of the others. It is usually this den that will serve as the place where she will give birth to her annual litter toward the end of next month.

The otter, like several other members of the weasel family, experiences a process of delayed implantation. This means that after mating, her fertilized eggs will enter a dormant period rather than become implanted in the walls of her uterus and develop as embryos.

Breeding season for the otter is generally in April, one to two weeks after the young are born. The fertilized eggs, known at this point as *blastocysts,* remain inactive until late January or very early February, when the two-month-long process of embryonic development starts.

Much is still unknown about the breeding behavior of the otter and its life in the wilds, especially during this season. For wildlife researchers, winter is a time when the movements of many land-dwelling creatures can be easily followed, as tracks in the snow provide a perfect record of their travels and encounters. For this playful aquatic weasel, winter's ice will undoubtedly help to keep many facets of its wild existence a secret for years to come.

The Elusive Fisher

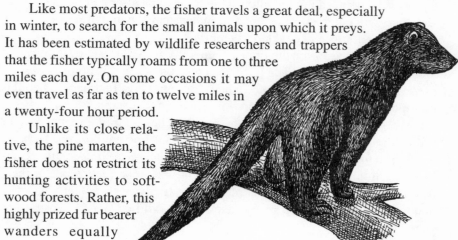

If an estimate were made of the number and abundance of the species of Adirondack wildlife based on a summer hike or canoe trip, a winter snowshoe venture or ski tour, the figure would be exceptionally low. Because most mammals are extremely wary of humans, the chance of an encounter with a wild animal in the Adirondacks is small. All creatures have keen senses that alert them well in advance that a person is approaching, causing them to quickly retreat into the background before they can be detected by a passerby.

One animal that is believed to be abundant in the Adirondacks, yet which is rarely seen because of its wary nature and secretive habits, is the fisher. This dark brown to nearly black furred member of the weasel family is about the size of a house cat. Its tail is slightly more bushy than a cat's, although it is about the same length and is held slightly upward. On those rare occasions when it is seen, the fisher is sometimes mistaken for this domestic pet.

Sportsmen who have witnessed the fisher startled by a dog say it arches its back and raises its hairs along its dorsal side, much as a house cat does when threatened. Such canine-fisher meetings are exceptionally rare, however, as this deep woods weasel ordinarily is very much aware of the presence of intruders and will flee the scene before a confrontation can occur.

Like most predators, the fisher travels a great deal, especially in winter, to search for the small animals upon which it preys. It has been estimated by wildlife researchers and trappers that the fisher typically roams from one to three miles each day. On some occasions it may even travel as far as ten to twelve miles in a twenty-four hour period.

Unlike its close relative, the pine marten, the fisher does not restrict its hunting activities to softwood forests. Rather, this highly prized fur bearer wanders equally through the vast deciduous woodlands of the Adirondacks and the dense stands of conifers. As a result, you may notice a set of fisher tracks almost anywhere when on an outdoor excursion during winter.

A fisher has five toes on each foot, making its imprint easily distinguishable from that of the four toe imprint of the coyote, fox, bobcat, or domestic dog. A fisher's paw, however, is similar in size to that of these other creatures, measuring approximately two and a half inches in diameter. Because of its lanky stature and the manner in which it hops along, the footprints of the fisher usually occur in pairs. Under normal conditions, each closely spaced set of paw prints is about two to three feet apart.

A half century or so ago, when it was legal to hunt the fisher, sportsmen would often follow a fresh set of its tracks for many miles hoping to jump one and get a clear shot at it. Most encounters would come when the fisher was feeding, but the ever alert and wary nature of the creature, known then as the pekan, made sneaking up on it a formidable task. In most cases the elusive fisher remained well ahead of its human pursuer and only fleeting glimpses of it were ever obtained. Such a hunt, although often fruitless, was considered to be worth the effort. During the early part of the 1900's, a fisher pelt, in prime condition, could bring in well over a hundred dollars, an extraordinary sum of money in that era.

An important process in the body of the female fisher is triggered by the increasing amount of daylight in mid- to late February. At this time of year, the embryos that were conceived nearly ten and a half months ago become implanted in the uterus and begin to develop. The fisher will give birth to its litter of from two to four young any time from mid-March until early April. In a week to ten days following birth, the female will quickly come into heat and breed again. The embryos that are formed do not develop past the blastocyst stage. These structures then lie dormant within the female until this time next year, when they will again grow into fetuses.

The chances are slim that you will ever see a fisher when traveling through the Adirondack wilderness. Though there is a healthy population of these handsome weasels roaming the woodlands, they tend to spot you first and disappear before you can see them.

A Spring Odor Arrives

Though miserable weather still occurs, winter does begin to loosen its icy grip on the Adirondacks in mid- to late February. Around the time of President's Day, the average daily temperatures gradually begin to warm, and daylight increases noticeably.

One of the first signs of the coming season is the return of the cutting odor of a skunk permeating the night air. On calm evenings, when the temperature remains in the teens or twenties, it is not unusual to smell the neighborhood skunk again on the prowl.

In the Adirondacks, generally around the third week of February, the skunk starts to arise from its long period of winter dormancy. Even though the weather at this time of year may not be much better than that of mid-January or early February, this chubby member of the weasel family is no longer content to remain asleep at night. It is the first of the region's prolonged sleepers to respond to the gradual changing of the seasons.

During the inevitable spells of bitter cold, when the mercury drops into the single digits or lower, or when blustery winds howl after sunset, this black and white nocturnal creature will remain in its den until conditions improve.

If the weather is not bad, skunks will leave their dens at night for the purpose of finding a mate. Late February to early March is their breeding season, and an awakening mating urge is the stimulus that causes this weasel to return to an active existence. Females tend to remain in their 100 to 250 acre territory during this time of year and let the males find them. It is not unusual for a male skunk to wander three to five miles a night during the latter portion of winter in its search for a mate.

Although mating is their prime concern in early March, food is still important. Skunks are scavengers at this time of year and remain so until mid- to late April. During the warmer months, the skunk feeds on an assortment of bugs, worms, eggs, small animals, leaves, and berries. In late winter and early spring, before most of these items become available again, this omnivorous weasel is forced to rely on any type of dead matter that it may happen to stumble upon, including food scraps contained in trash bags.

During its winter dormancy, a skunk's body continues to produce the pungent smelling musk for which it is so infamous. This milky-white chemical is stored in a pair of scent glands located near the base of its tail. As a result, during the first few weeks following its emergence from winter sleep, these sacs are as full as can be, and the skunk seldom hesitates to use its most effective means of self-defense.

Later, during the spring and throughout the summer, the skunk uses this foul odor to dissuade an attacker only as a last resort. The slow daily rate at which the chemical is produced does not allow the skunk an endless supply of musk. Discharging the substance as little as two to three times an evening over a period of a week can seriously deplete its reserves. Consequently, after re-educating the potentially hostile creatures in its territory (like the neighbor's dog) shortly after emerging from its dormant period, the skunk begins to use its lingering scent much more sparingly.

Unlike most Adirondack animals, the skunk is equally at home in the village or in the wilderness woodlands. A hole that exists under a porch or beneath a backyard shed is every bit as attractive to this mammal as is a hillside burrow near some remote forest clearing. Don't be too surprised to see one of these slow moving animals meandering over a snowbank or note the odor of a skunk seeping into your living room late some evening.

While it is too early to worry about having a can of bug repellent nearby, or a fly swatter to get rid of a pesky yellow jacket or hornet, it is not too early to have that extra can of tomato juice in the back of the refrigerator, just in case someone in the family (usually a pet) has an unfortunate close encounter of the skunk kind.

Mating Time for the Red Fox

Besides the skunk, there are several other mammals whose breeding seasons begin during the latter half of February. The red squirrel and coyote both start to seek out mates around this time. Also, as previously described, the breeding season for the beaver reaches its peak during mid-February. Another creature that alters its winter routine at this time of year in response to an elevated level of reproductive hormones is the red fox.

The resident male fox begins to seek out the female that also occupies his territory. Usually this is the same animal he mated with the previous year. This is done both by reading the scents in the air and following her tracks until he encounters her. Foxes also communicate their presence to one another, especially at this time of year, by vocalizations. The red fox produces a variety of high-pitched yelping barks that can carry for over a half mile on a clear night.

Like the coyote and other fox species, this rusty-tan wild dog, especially the adult male, is a territorial creature. The size of its land claim depends entirely on the availability of food in that area. In places where there is an abundant supply of rodents, other small animals, berries, fruits, and insects the omnivorous red fox may range over an area of less than 200 acres. These settings may be abandoned fields, along the edges of open woodlands, or near the shores of swamps and marshes.

In the dense, unbroken forests that cover so much of the Adirondacks, food for the red fox is more scarce. It is estimated by some wildlife researchers that the red fox must maintain a home range of over a thousand acres in wilderness areas in order to satisfy its food demands.

As is the case with many other territorial creatures, the red fox advertises its claim to a particular piece of real estate with scent posts. By placing its urine and feces in special spots, this creature is able to denote ownership of that particular place. Because this dog has such a highly developed sense of smell, a wandering juvenile in search of a territory is unlikely to miss a scent post, or be unaware that it is trespassing in an area occupied by another male.

The sheer size of the area occupied by most red foxes in the Adirondacks often allows an intruding male the opportunity to meander across another's property, and even remain there for some time before being discovered. Since the body of each fox produces a unique scent, the owner will eventually come across the scent trail produced by an unwelcome visitor. While food is particularly important during winter, the presence of an interloper is of even greater concern during the breeding season. As a result, once such a trail is noticed, the intruder is immediately tracked down and confronted by the owner.

Upon encountering a trespasser, a red fox will first show its displeasure with a series of body postures, such as standing rigid and holding its ears as high as possible. It then bares its teeth, usually causing the trespassing fox to beat a hasty retreat. Seldom do these wild animals actually resort to a fight, and, if they do, the chances are that they will not seriously injure one another.

While one male will not tolerate the presence of another in its home range, it is believed that any vixen is allowed to enter and roam about an area without interference from the resident male. Ordinarily, only the female that mates with the owner of a particular hillside or valley ends up sharing that area with him. It is not known for certain if the vixen which occupies a given area will repel another female in search of a place to establish her home range. In any event, usually just one male and one female occupy the same general space. Although the two foxes may share a given territory, they will usually have little to do with each other from early autumn, the time when the family of the previous year begins to go its own separate ways, until now.

While the two still do not hunt for food together, the male begins to spend increasingly greater amounts of time with his mate during early February. The courtship period may last for several weeks before the vixen enters her very brief heat period. It is said by fox researchers that the female is receptive for only two to three days; however, as she nears this critical time, she notifies her mate by the emission of certain odors. As a result, the male is certain to be with her when the proper time comes.

It is difficult to say for sure how severe the weather will be over the next several weeks. Yet one thing is definite: male foxes have more on their minds than simply putting up with February's cold temperatures and attempting to find enough food.

The Voice of the Forest

To avoid attracting attention to themselves, most mammals do not produce frequent or loud vocalizations. Although all mammals are capable of making some type of sound, these noises tend to be reserved only for special occasions. For example, communication between a mother and her young is often accomplished with some type of sound. Breeding season is also a time when the instinct to remain silent and inconspicuous is overpowered by the desire to advertise one's presence to a prospective mate. In the Adirondacks, there is no other creature as willing to make noise as the red squirrel.

This rusty-tan colored rodent will also use its vocal abilities to proclaim sole ownership of a particular one or two acre parcel of the forest. For the red squirrel, territorial ownership is constantly maintained by a series of loud chattering sounds that should be familiar to anyone that spends time outdoors in the Adirondacks. Because of the willingness of the red squirrel to sneak into a neighbor's territory and take advantage of food resources there, this agile tree dweller frequently notifies its neighbors that it is watching and that no incursion will be tolerated.

As its breeding season draws near in late February, male red squirrels develop a strong desire to stray from the confines of their home range to search for females that are in their brief heat period. It is not unusual, therefore, to see a strange red squirrel at the bird feeder during this time of year (provided you can distinguish an outsider from the one that regularly sits there and gorges itself on your sunflower seeds). This movement causes a heightened level of turmoil and a corresponding increase in the chatter that is used to dissuade intruders.

Edgy occupants during this season may not only voice their anger at a neighboring red squirrel that has come too near a boundary, but at any creature of the forest that happens to cross into a "restricted area." Even humans may get a heated scolding from an upset red squirrel if they should happen to appear in the wrong place. By late March, breeding activities generally fade and there is a return to a more normal level of chatter.

Five and a half weeks after mating, the female gives birth to a litter that averages three or four in number. Baby red squirrels are slow to develop. It takes three and a half weeks before their eyes open and another week before they are ready to take their first steps out of the nest. They seldom venture far into the canopy alone, even after they become mobile. Typically, the young remain under the watchful eye of their mother for the rest of the spring and into early summer.

Although a female with young tends to refrain from vocalizing when her babies are near her, she will not hesitate to verbally assault any animal or person that is too close to a nest sheltering her young.

Some red squirrels will breed a second time during the year. In the Adirondacks, this usually occurs in late June, about the same time that school is getting out for the summer. An increase in the level of verbal commotion may be detected at this time as well.

By bearing a second litter each year, nature has seen to it that there will always be red squirrels around to frustrate those clever minded individuals who attempt to make squirrel-proof bird feeders. It also ensures the constant chatter that is as characteristic of the Adirondacks as is the call of the loon.

Snow Fleas

On those calm, sunny, late winter days, when the temperature rises into the 40's, subtle signs of spring appear. The early morning stillness is periodically broken by the "Feee-Be-Be" call of the chickadees, indicating the rapid approach of their mating season. The boisterous chattering of red squirrels and the loud squawking of blue jays also become more noticeable with each passing day. Small flocks of crows may be seen flying overhead or perched atop a tall white pine. From these lofty positions, crows can survey the area for the thawing remains of winter-killed animals that appear as the snow gradually fades. Melting snow and ice also increase the humidity, and by midday the air takes on a distinctively fresh fragrance.

As the day progresses and the moisture content of the snow increases, tiny black specks begin to appear on its surface. These may be especially noticeable in a footprint or a depression created some time ago. In some places, particularly close to the base of a rough-barked tree, or near a rotting, moss-covered stump, holes in the snow may turn nearly black.

A close examination of these darkened depressions reveals hundreds, even thousands, of tiny black entities hopping and jumping about. These are the snow fleas, the first of the insects to resurrect themselves after their winter dormancy and considered by some naturalists to be among the most abundant of soil insects in the Adirondacks.

Snow fleas are not related to the group of parasitic pests that most people ordinarily think of when they hear the word "flea." Rather, these minute jumping bugs belong to a primitive category of insects known as springtails.

Springtails get their name from the pronged appendage extending from their abdomen that enables them to jump. Properly known as a *furca*, this stiff tail bends under their body before springing down and out, propelling them upward.

Because the body structures of the springtails are so different from all other insects, some entomologists are reluctant to classify them as insects. For example, these tiny creatures have no wings. Although there are other insects that are unable to fly, nearly all have at least a rudimentary set or two of these appendages on their thorax. Also, unlike nearly every other insect, the springtails do not experience any metamorphic change during their life cycle. Upon emerging from their microscopic eggs, the young bugs are miniature versions of the adults.

Another basic difference between the springtails and other insects is their manner of reproduction. Rather than mating directly with a female, the male springtails simply deposit sperm on the ground in small, scattered droplets. Because they are so abundant, the chances are good that a female will soon come along and walk over one of these droplets, thereby introducing the sperm onto her body.

Like other primitive land dwelling organisms, the springtails have a thin, soft skin that does not hold water well. Dehydration is, therefore, one of the greatest threats confronting these tiny creatures. This is why snow fleas become active only when there is an ample moisture content to the snow or in the layer of humus covering the ground.

Since snow fleas can jump only about an inch, a depression in the snow several inches deep can entrap them. After an hour or two, a hole in the snow may collect a hundred of more of these prolific bugs. As the late afternoon approaches and the temperature cools, the snow fleas abandon any attempt to leap out and begin to work their way down into the snow. Because of their extremely small size, they are able to crawl through the spaces that exist between snow grains.

During periods of sub-freezing temperatures, snow fleas, like other soil-dwelling bugs, simply lie dormant in the layer of humus on the ground. Some are also known to seek shelter under the bark of trees, especially the

32

maple, cherry, and pine.

Despite their small size, snow fleas play a significant role in the ecology of wooded areas. Their incessant appetite for the bits and pieces of dead matter that covers the forest floor helps in the conversion of this material into nutrients which can be used by plants. Snow fleas, in turn, are eaten by a wide array of small predatory bugs, such as spiders and miniature carnivorous beetles, becoming an important part of the forest's food web.

The next time you are outdoors on one of those days that cause a case of spring fever, you might want to look closely at the snow's surface to see if you can detect one of these common, but often overlooked, harbingers of spring.

The Return of the Raccoon

In the Adirondacks, typically around the first or second week of March, regular breaks start to occur in the seemingly continuous pattern of winter weather. These frequent, brief spells of early spring, and the lengthening of the day, act as a catalyst in altering the wintertime routine of numerous forms of wildlife.

White-tailed deer, for instance, begin to wander from their wintering yards, and if the snow is not too deep, head back to their summer range. Birds stray further from the feeders that helped support them over the past several months to re-explore areas that were seldom visited during the middle of winter. The beaver attempts to break out of its confinement below the ice by squeezing through holes that form along south-facing shores, or where a small stream flows into its pond, or near the spillway on its dam. A chipmunk may temporarily leave its shelter for a short span of time on mild, sunny days to check on the status of its territory. The emergence of spring at the beginning of March also causes the raccoon to awaken and leave its den, often for the first time in several months.

As is the case with several other Adirondack animals, the raccoon experiences a desire to mate during late winter. Although the female may stray from her den, it is the male that does most of the traveling at this time of year, searching for a mate. Occasionally, a male may happen upon a female that is accompanied by her cubs from the previous year. In this case, he will not only mate with the mother, but also with any of the females in the litter that may be reaching sexual maturity. In the Adirondacks, most raccoons remain reproductively undeveloped until either much later in the spring, or until they near the age of two.

While the urge to breed is a primary factor motivating the raccoon to an active life, hunger also becomes a force in causing this masked creature to leave its den. Yet, while the raccoon may lumber about its quarter of a square mile home range looking for food, the chances are that it will find very little to eat in March. Unless it happens to stumble upon the thawing carcass of an animal that died in winter, or encounters a bag of garbage near the street, it will return to its den with an empty stomach. Stored fat accumulated during the late summer and fall still remain its principle source of energy at this time of year.

It has been determined by several researchers that the raccoon loses nearly half of its autumn weight by the time it begins to feed regularly, which in the Adirondacks is usually mid-April. During periods of cold, blustery weather, the raccoon will abandon any feeding or breeding ventures and attempt to conserve as much of its remaining fat as possible by curling up in its den and sleeping away the time until weather conditions improve.

During April, as the snow disappears and the ground begins to thaw, nighttime foraging trips become increasingly more common and far more productive. Earthworms that come to the surface after dusk are routinely caught by this nimble-fingered animal. Frogs, peepers, salamanders, and crayfish are also caught, since the raccoon spends much of its time prowling the edges of recently thawed waterways turning over stones and checking under shoreline debris for small forms of animal life to eat. The tender shoots of newly sprouting plants, such as the fiddleheads of various ferns, are also eagerly eaten. Beetles, crickets, grasshoppers, and other bugs emerging from their winter dormancy help to appease its appetite.

35

Later in April, the nests of birds, such as the red-winged blackbird, may be plundered for the tasty eggs they contain. Pools of shallow water are checked for minnows and shiners, which the raccoon is able to hook with its sharp front claws.

During mid-April, along with finding food, the raccoon may also be looking for a new place to live. The cubs which the female raised the year before usually remain with her in her den throughout the winter. However, as her time to give birth to a new litter draws near, she becomes less accepting of her yearling cubs. In the Adirondacks, this dispersal of maturing raccoons usually occurs around the second or third week of April. A large cavity in the trunk of a tree is the site most highly favored, but occasionally a raccoon will set up housekeeping in the attic of an abandoned cabin, or among the rafters of an unused garage. Wood duck nest boxes have also been known to attract yearling raccoons looking for a den. Hollow logs lying on the ground, empty woodchuck burrows, or rock cubbies on boulder-strewn hillsides may also be used as denning sites if the raccoon is unable to find anything that it can climb and take up residence within.

Because it is not a territorial creature, a raccoon will tolerate other raccoons living within the area over which it ranges. In places where food is plentiful, such as along the edges of marshes, the banks of rivers, and shores of ponds, several raccoons may live within one general area. They tend to steer clear of one another, however, as the raccoon is not known for its sociability.

While it may be several weeks to a month before spring weather becomes the rule rather than the exception, it is not too early to have a garbage can tipped over during the night by this masked marauder. If you live on the outskirts of a town, near a lake, pond, or river, you will undoubtedly be visited sooner or later by a rather thin looking, coarse-haired creature hoping to find a scrap of food and perhaps a place to settle down for the rest of the season.

A Dangerous Time for the Snowshoe Hare

While the outbreaks of spring weather may be a welcome occurrence for many creatures, temporary mild spells are often disastrous for the varying hare, better known as the snowshoe rabbit. Throughout most of the winter, the snow in the Adirondacks tends to be deep and fluffy. The powdery texture of winter's white blanket strongly favors the snowshoe hare. With its enlarged hind feet, this animal, which belongs to a group called *lagomorphs*, can more easily travel over the snowbound landscape than any other wildlife resident of the northwoods. Its agility through dense underbrush and its jumping ability allow this hare to easily outmaneuver any forest predator that would enjoy dining on its flesh.

Yet the alternating battle between masses of cold arctic air and warm, temperate weather systems during March results in a substantial change in the condition of the snow. Late winter thaws cause high levels of water to develop in the snow which inevitably freezes when a Canadian high weather pattern descends over the northeast. The resulting crust is usually strong enough to support the weight of animals having smaller paws. Foxes, fishers, coyotes, bobcats, and weasels are now able to bound across the surface about as easily as their snowshoe prey. This greatly evens the odds in a chase between these predators and the hare.

Southerly breezes during March, especially toward the end of the month, bring the return of another hare enemy, the hawk. At a time when an attack from the ground is likely, the varying hare must also be ever alert against an aerial assault from a red-tailed, red-shoulder, or broad-winged hawk. As if this were not enough, a snowshoe rabbit may additionally be attacked, beaten up, and sometimes even killed by neighboring varying hares during March.

In late January and most of February, male varying hares become gregarious, tending to congregate and "hang out" in small groups. During this time they frequently chase one another, especially at night when they are most active. Researchers, observing them on clear, moonlit evenings, have noted them leaping wildly when together and even jumping over one another as if playing a game of leap frog.

As March arrives and their mating season rapidly approaches, playfulness quickly turns to aggressiveness. A male encountering another male will attempt to drive it from the immediate area by punching with its front legs, biting with its sharp incisors, and kicking with its powerful hind legs. Because this species of hare has a relatively thin and delicate hide, such an attack can result in serious injury to one or both animals. On occasion, a male has been known to kill a rival during such battles.

The larger and stronger males tend to travel about more and may venture from their home range in search of females. Although the males begin to search out females during the first week in March, it is not until around St. Patrick's Day that the females become receptive to their advances.

As in cottontail rabbits, the process of mating, bearing young, and raising the litter is one that continues throughout the spring and into mid-summer. At least two litters are born each year, though three are more typical in the Adirondacks. There are reports that under favorable conditions a varying hare can even bear four litters in a season, though this probably does not occur very often. Litter size can be from a single individual to seven or eight. It has been estimated by wildlife biologists that two to three births per litter is the average.

The high reproductive rate for which rabbits and hares are so well known is a great help in off-setting their high mortality rate. Approximately two-thirds of the young end up as a meal for some type of predator during their first year of life. Though after the first year the odds for survival improve, they are still not dramatically higher. A realistic life span for those that reach their first birthday is said to be around three to four years. Because of its many natural enemies, life for these furry, long-eared creatures is filled with danger, especially during the March season of crusty snow.

The Return of the Black Duck

As warmer temperatures and a more intense sun act on the snow, the run-off of water raises the level of small streams and strengthens the force of the current. This flushes away most of the ice that built up in winter and prevents re-freezing during the spells of cold that regularly occur in March.

The extensive stretches of open water that form along alder-choked brooks and in marshlands adjacent to meandering rivers is enough to entice the return of the black duck. Despite the winter weather in March, this exceptionally wary bird is quick to return to its northern breeding ground during the first few weeks of this month.

Since its thick covering of down is coated with a protective oil, its plumage remains dry and warm despite the constant exposure to the water. Additionally, an insulating layer of fat helps this dark-colored waterfowl retain body heat when paddling in the near-freezing water.

While the shoreline may still be snowbound in early March and useless as a place for foraging, the pockets of open water that exist, especially in the shallows, harbor a more than adequate supply of food. Small, dormant invertebrates that winter in quiet aquatic areas are abundant and easy for this bird to filter from the bottom sediment. Another important and plentiful source of food are the seeds of last year's water plants.

Unlike the mallard, its very close relative, the black duck tends to avoid aquatic areas which exist close to places of human activity. But any type of remote setting, such as a beaver pond, an aldered brook, an isolated cattail marsh or pond, the backwater of a large river, or even a spruce bog, can serve as a home to this bird.

The ability of the black duck to adapt to a wide variety of aquatic ecosystems is one of the main reasons why it has been so successful in the wilds. The many remote bodies of fresh water relatively free of human disturbances make the black duck one of the most abundant species of waterfowl in the Adirondacks.

Black ducks have strong homing instincts directing them back to the area they left the previous year. Once they have returned to the general region, though, it may be several days to a week before they finally settle into the area that will serve as their home.

When black ducks arrive back in the North Country, they are already paired for the coming breeding season. The bond between a male and female usually develops during the early fall, just prior to their southward migration. In cases in which one of the partners is killed, either during the autumn journey south or on the wintering grounds, single birds attempt to find other mates before reaching their breeding territory.

For the first week or two, the pair will travel extensively in their home range, averaging a mile or two in diameter. When visiting different sites, the birds learn where the richest food supplies exist and where danger is least likely to occur. Eventually the pair of blacks will establish an attachment to a particular spot. This is the place they will go after feeding, when they want to rest. It is near this location that the hen usually elects to construct her nest for when the time comes in mid-to late April to lay her eggs.

Because of the diversity of habitats which the black duck occupies, its nest can be located almost anywhere, including a stand of conifers, a tangle of alders, a thicket of reeds and tall grasses, on the ground, on top of a mound of dead plants, on a rotted stump, or even in the crotch of a tree. Also, unlike many birds, the black duck is not territorial. As a result, the home range of one pair may overlap that of one or several others. This is why it is not unusual to see small flocks of these dark-colored ducks in one general area throughout the early spring.

Although putting away heavy jackets, taking the snow tires off the car, and raking the lawn are still some time away for humans, as far as this surface feeding duck is concerned, spring is here.

The Chipmunk Awakens

The shy and secretive habits of most wild animals, coupled with their desire to reside in remote places, make it difficult to detect changes that occur in their daily activities as spring draws near. On the other hand, a break in the wintertime routine of the chipmunk is more readily noted as a result of its friendly attitude towards humans and its willingness to live close to people.

While the chipmunk may be seen scampering across lawns and in and out of woodpiles throughout the warmer months of the year, their complete disappearance in October or early November indicates that they become dormant in winter. After descending into a chamber several feet below the surface, the chipmunk will curl up into a ball, wrap its tail over its body, and fall into a deep sleep.

Unlike the form of hibernation experienced by woodchucks, jumping mice, and bats, a chipmunk's state of inactivity is not as extreme or prolonged. Rather than sleep for months without stirring, this small, striped ground squirrel awakens once or twice a week. When it does, it makes short trips to a nearby chamber that houses the cache of seeds, beechnuts, and dried berries it assembled last summer and autumn. Since it doesn't develop a substantial deposit of fat to sustain itself for the approximately four months that it remains in its burrow, the chipmunk must periodically awaken to eat.

Except for one or two brief trips to the surface during a mid-winter thaw, the chipmunk will not leave the confines of its subterranean complex of tunnels and rooms. With the arrival of warm sunny days during the middle of this month, it removes the earthen plug from one of its entrance holes in order to make sporadic visits to the world above. These trips tend to be of short duration, and seldom does this rodent stray far from its hole, particularly if a substantial covering of snow remains on the ground.

Stops are usually made at those places where food was obtained during the previous year. If it uncovers something to eat, it will feed again and then gather a mouthful or two of food to haul back to its burrow. Like a miser with gold, the chipmunk is always looking to add to its stockpile of seeds, especially after its reserve has been depleted during the winter.

After returning to its burrow, the chipmunk retires to its sleeping chamber and again drifts into a state of deep sleep for several more days. It is not until the early part of April that it finally begins to awaken daily and regularly come to the surface. Even then, a trip out of its bur-

41

row will be abandoned if the weather proves to be too cold or snowy.

It is also during the early part of April that male chipmunks begin to wander well beyond their territory to search for females that are coming into heat. It has been reported by researchers that the female is receptive for a period of only several hours to half a day. It is also believed that the female will emit a certain scent just prior to becoming fertile, advertising her condition to the males of the area.

After breeding, the female retires to the comfort of her burrow. Depending on weather conditions and the availability of food, she may not leave her nest for some time to come. The male chipmunk, however, continues his daily search for other breeding partners.

It is a full month after mating that the young are born. The litter size is said to average four or five births, and their rate of development is rather slow. It is not until they are six weeks old that they finally venture from one of the main tunnel entrances. Once they reach this stage, these squeaky-voiced rodents rapidly become independent. Within ten days from the time they emerge into the world of light, the young chipmunks stray from their mother's care to establish a territory of their own and settle into a solitary existence.

This increase in the chipmunk population may be noted in the very late spring by the increase in the number of them scurrying across the yard or driveway and around the woodpile. This is in sharp contrast to mid-March, when sightings are few and limited almost exclusively to those days that produce a severe case of spring fever in the chipmunk and in people.

A Night Dweller

Of all groups of animals found in the Adirondacks, none are as well-known as the squirrels. Because these ubiquitous creatures live in close proximity to humans, they are a familiar sight to area residents and visitors alike. There is, however, one common member of this family of rodents that does not share its relatives highly visible profile. Despite its numbers, a willingness to live near people's houses, and a fondness for eating from bird feeders, the flying squirrel is among the least known or studied forms of wildlife.

The nocturnal habits of this animal are the main reason why the flying squirrel is so rarely seen. It is only after sunset, when darkness conceals its presence, that this chipmunk-size creature emerges from its treetop retreat. Its exceptionally large eyes enable it to see well under dimly lit conditions, such as overcast nights or during times of a new moon.

Despite its name, this elusive creature is unable to fly in the manner of birds and bats. The flying squirrel can float gently downward because a thin membrane which connects its front and hind legs, when outstretched, acts like the wing of a glider. This action allows it to quickly move through the forest canopy by parachuting from the upper section of one tree to the lower portion of another. This membrane does not, however, allow the squirrel to fly in an upward direction. This gliding talent is in contrast to the ability of the more conspicuous members of its family to leap from branch to branch.

Because the membrane impedes its movement on the ground, especially in places covered by tall, dense weeds and grasses, the flying squirrel spends more of its time in trees than any other Adirondack mammal. Though it does periodically venture to the forest floor in search of fallen seeds, soil bugs, and mushrooms, much of its foraging is done among the limbs and twigs of the canopy.

When searching for food, the flying squirrel is less selective than any other squirrel or rodent. While the seeds of both hardwoods and conifers are the staple items in its diet, this omnivorous animal also consumes a substantial quantity of insects, bird eggs, and spiders. Some naturalists think that the flying squirrel will even attack, kill, and eat small mice and voles when given the opportunity.

Like its red and gray relatives, the flying squirrel is also fond of sunflower seeds. Its visits to bird feeders, however, often go unnoticed. Either it is just too dark to see this nighttime marauder, or its raids come after everyone has gone to bed.

43

When around homes, camps, or lean-tos, the flying squirrel usually is less wary than any other animal. Some naturalists believe that the flying squirrel is easier to tame than its striped relative, the chipmunk. It may closely approach a person and, with relative ease, can be coaxed into taking peanuts from your hand.

While the flying squirrel occasionally takes up residence in wooded areas inside Adirondack villages, it is much more at home in mature forests. A setting where there is a mixture of hardwoods and softwoods, especially hemlock, sugar maple, and yellow birch, is strongly preferred. Additionally, places with an abundance of tree cavities well off the ground tend to support large populations of the flying squirrel.

In the places where flying squirrels abound, it is believed that several individuals may occupy the same nest during the height of winter. Like other tree squirrels, this mammal does not hibernate; yet, like its close relatives, it will become briefly inactive during periods of extreme cold and blustery weather. The huddling together of a few neighbors in one nest helps conserve body heat and is one means by which this solitary creature combats frequent outbreaks of arctic air.

With the arrival of March, such gregarious behavior is quickly abandoned, regardless of the severity of the weather. As with so many other animals, late winter is the breeding season for the flying squirrel, and during this time territorial boundaries are more passionately defended.

Despite its friendly temperament toward humans, few studies of this common Adirondack squirrel's habits and life in the trees have been made. Consequently, little is known about its breeding behavior and mating rituals. What is known is that the young are born sometime in April or early May and that they are reared entirely by the female. It takes approximately five weeks for the babies to develop to the stage where they are able to wander out of their nest, which is usually located in a tree cavity well above the forest floor.

It is during the time when they are out of the nest that these immature creatures are most vulnerable. While exploring the canopy many fall victim to owls and, while foraging through debris on the ground, to predators such as foxes and coyotes.

Although they are seldom seen, tracks of this mammal can be noted around a feeder after an early evening snowfall has removed all traces of daytime visitors. Unquestionably, the best chance of catching a glimpse of a flying squirrel is on a clear night in late winter when the light of a full

44

moon is intensified by a fresh covering of snow, and the mercury is not dropping too far out of sight. On such evenings, this nocturnal forest resident might be seen moving along a branch overhead or sailing out of a tall tree to a recently stocked feeder.

The Return of the Red-Winged Blackbird

It is not too long after the first day of spring that small, noisy flocks of red-winged blackbirds begin to arrive in the North Country. They are attracted by the bare ground that begins to show through on south-facing slopes and in open, wind-swept fields and marshes around the time of the vernal equinox.

The older males are the first to return. While some of these are transients, waiting a few days until conditions for further northward migration become favorable again, others are ready to re-establish a territory in the same general area they left the year before. Like most birds, this common harbinger of spring possesses a strong attachment to the area in which it previously lived. However, each spring, every bird will attempt to improve its breeding territory by laying claim to a better site.

The first birds back claim the best spots, but these sites are not easy to keep. The occupant must be ready to defend his territory against all late-comers. The "o-ka-tee" call, often heard from a marsh in the spring, is made by a male red-winged blackbird announcing it will not tolerate intruders. Exposing or flashing the reddish-yellow epaulets on its upper wing, and fanning its tail feathers are other means the bird uses to express its anger and intent to de-

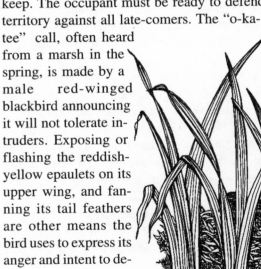

45

fend its chosen site.

Fierce conflicts often arise in the spring among males competing for the same breeding territory, or between neighbors that have not settled on the exact location of a boundary. In addition to verbal battles and plumage displays, one bird may dive at an intruder in order to chase him from the area. Sometimes the birds bite and peck at one another in an attempt to hold a piece of real estate. The older birds (four to seven-year-olds) typically win the disputes for the most highly prized territories. Generally, the two and three-year-old males end up with whatever space is left.

Much of the fighting among the breeding males dies down by early April as exact boundaries gradually become established. Soon after, however, a new wave of conflict arises when the females arrive. Again, the individuals that are the first to return take the choice nesting spots. As more females appear, the fighting between them increases, with each trying to prevent encroachment by the surrounding birds. Female red-winged blackbirds establish their territory within an area controlled by a particular male. Because the female needs less space than the male, two or three females usually occupy an area held by a single male.

By mid-April, most of the females have returned and settled into their nesting areas. As calm starts to return and mating is about to begin, the year-old males arrive and spark a fresh round of noise and commotion. Because they are not yet ready to breed, these yearlings are driven out by both males whose territory they have invaded, and by the females that wish to get mating underway. This forces the yearlings to spend the entire spring and summer on the periphery of the breeding grounds or in fields and pastures far from the mature birds.

While the red-winged blackbird is extremely intolerant of others when on the breeding ground (except for its mate), its attitude towards its neighbors is different when away from the marsh. When it ventures into fields and meadows to pick up seeds, the bird is quite gregarious, usually forming tight flocks. Also, when a predator such as a hawk, crow, or weasel has been noticed lurking in the immediate area, the red-winged blackbird is known to band together with one or more of its nearby rivals in a joint effort to drive away the enemy.

A human passing near or through a marsh occupied by red-winged blackbirds is not given a warm welcome either. Early season canoeists paddling near a dense section of cattails may be subjected to the verbal wrath of these possessive but striking red-winged birds.

The First Bird to Nest

In March, most of the birds that breed in the Adirondacks have yet to return, or are only now starting to arrive en masse and will not be ready to nest for at least several weeks. There is, however, one permanent avian resident of the region that has already entered into its courtship period. Beginning around the first or second week of March, the barred owl experiences an awakening mating urge.

The approach of this owl's breeding season, as with that of nearly any other bird, can be noted by the increased regularity of its calls. Vocalizations are used by birds to affirm their hold on a particular parcel of land and to draw the attention of the females that reside within its boundaries. Although the hooting call of this nocturnal bird of prey may be heard at any time of the day, it is more common in the late afternoon, early evening, and during pre-sunrise hours.

While the great horned owl also makes a hooting sound, it is the call of the barred owl that most people normally associate with these robust, round-faced birds. Their echoing song is composed of two sets of four hoots apiece. There are several phrases that are used to describe this eight-note song, but the one "Who cooks for you, who cooks for you all " perhaps best represents the beat of this call. The last note of this monotone song is noticeably longer than the first seven and also drops off in pitch. (Both the screech owl and saw-whet owl make a whistling-beeping sound, rather than a hooting call.)

Because it prefers to reside in mature stands of timber, especially in mixed forests, the barred owl is the most common of the three species of owls existing in the Adirondacks. Aging stands of trees, so common throughout the Forest Preserve, typically contain numerous large diameter trunks that are partially rotted near the top and which have suitable nesting cavities for this owl.

Like most other owls, the barred owl is inept at building a nest. For this reason it usually tries to find an appropriate size hole in a tree, which it lines with a few feathers before laying its two or three brown eggs. If its nest from the previous year is still intact, this early breeder will reoccupy it. (In one study, a naturalist observed a pair of barred owls nesting in the exact same cavity for a span of ten years.) If the previous year's nest is no longer usable, the barred owl must then search the forest for a new cavity. If one cannot be located, the bird will try to find an abandoned crow or squirrel nest which is in good condition and ready for immediate occupancy.

The barred owl may also take over a nest made in previous seasons by a red-shouldered hawk. Both of these birds of prey hunt and nest in similar settings. Since the barred owl begins to nest well before this diurnal predator, it does not encounter any resistance in laying claim to the hawk's structure. Upon returning to its former nesting site, the red-shouldered hawk, rather than expelling the owl, simply constructs a new twig and stick platform, often in the same area. This is why both barred owls and red-shouldered hawks have been observed nesting in very close proximity to one another.

While the barred owl coexists nicely with the red-shouldered hawk, it does not get along so well with its larger, tufted-eared relative, the great horned owl. This more aggressive owl often displaces the barred owl, especially from marginal woodland settings where the availability of nesting sites may be severely limited. However, in the dense forests of the Adirondacks, the great horned owl seems to be more tolerant of its smaller cousin.

The great horned owl is not the only bird that will attack the barred owl. Crows and blue jays also are well known for flying around, diving at, and harassing this owl. In order to minimize the threat of being mobbed by these other birds, the barred owl will roost during the day in thick stands of evergreens. There, it usually perches on a limb near the trunk. Its mottled gray and brown plumage causes it to blend into the dimly lit, shadowy background of needles, twigs, and sunlight, making it very difficult for other creatures to notice.

Shortly after it locates a

safe spot in which to nest, usually in the same place as last year, the barred owl is ready to mate and lay its eggs. This typically occurs in the Adirondacks at the very beginning of April. Because it nests so early in the year, its young hatch, develop, and are ready to leave the nest around the same time that immature mice, voles and other small rodents are leaving theirs. Since the immature owls learn to hunt at a time when there is an abundance of young, inexperienced prey wandering over the forest floor, the task of learning how to swoop down and catch a small rodent is immeasurably easier.

Although it will be some months more before young owls are prowling the forests for mice, by early April the learning process has already begun.

Maple Sugaring Season

Early spring in the Adirondacks is a time of awakening. During March and early April, raccoons, chipmunks, woodchucks, and bears begin to rouse from their long winter sleep. Bugs that winter under the bark of trees, in hollow trunks, or on the ground beneath the layer of leaf litter in sheltered, snow-free places also begin to stir. As the weather starts to warm, trees also begin to awaken from their prolonged period of dormancy. Although they show little outward response to the first few warm spells of the new season, these woody plants do react when the daily temperatures finally push above freezing. Nowhere is this more evident than in a stand of tapped maple trees.

The awakening of a tree in early spring is marked by the return of the upward flow of sap through the trunk. Like blood vessels in our body, the cells that compose the bulk of a trunk are designed for transporting fluids and dissolved materials from the lower to the upper sections of a tree. In summer, since water absorbed by the roots is needed in the leaves to carry out the process of photosynthesis, vast quantities of sap, composed almost entirely of water, flow up the trunk to these green, food-producing structures.

In early spring, long before the leaves emerge, sugars are needed in the upper sections of the tree to nourish the slowly developing buds. On days when the temperatures rise above freezing, a sweetened sap moves upward through the outer rings of wood in the trunk.

Photosynthesis in summer causes trees to produce vast amounts of sugars. These molecules travel down the trunk for storage, either in special cells in the roots, or in microscopic tubes which radiate out from the center of the trunk.

In order to store these nutrients effectively, the sugars are converted into starches. This helps prevent spoilage during the heat of the summer and warm spells in autumn. Starches also permit the cells to decrease the amount of water they contain. This reduction in the concentration of water is essential in the preparation for winter when temperatures remain below freezing. After the trunk and roots become dormant during the autumn, and the ground freezes in early winter, the stored starches are gradually con-verted back to sugars.

The return of warmer weather during the late winter stimulates the tree, which causes the roots to become active and again begin absorbing water. Since frozen soil is unable to yield any moisture, only the roots ex-tending below the frost line are able to take in water.

50

During years with little snow cover, when the frost penetrates deep into the ground, the intake of water is limited, and the flow of sap is very slow to begin.

As the soil thaws, and melting snow saturates the ground, the amount of water absorbed by the roots increases. Inside the roots the sugars quickly dissolve in the water, creating a concentration in the cells that causes more water to be pulled into the roots. This additional intake of fluid creates a pressure that forces the sweetened sap up into the trunk and towards the branches. On nights when the temperature drops below freezing, the flow of sap in the twigs and outer sections of the trunk stops. However, in the soil which still remains above freezing, the roots continue to absorb water. This results in a substantial build-up of fluid pressure inside the roots as well as in the trunk of the tree. When the air temperature goes above freezing the next day, and as bright sunlight strikes and warms the trunk, the temporary blockage thaws and the inside pressure begins forcing the sap up the trunk at a fairly high rate. Periods of weather that produce cold, crisp nights and warm, sunny days, like those that typify the very end of March and the first half of April, are a maple syrup producer's delight.

It is not long after a good run of sap that the buds on the trees begin to swell ever so slightly. As they begin to react to the favorable temperatures, and respond to the increased level of nutrients, the buds gradually develop a reddish tint. This produces the subtle change in color that is noticed on a hardwood hillside beginning in late March. It is this change that indicates the slow awakening of the Adirondacks deciduous woodlands.

APRIL

The Mole

As the snow melts in April, athletic fields and mowed meadows often reveal a wide assortment of accumulated debris. Regardless of the amount of yard work done in autumn, there always seem to be leaves that should be raked, twigs that have to be removed, and papers that need to be picked up. Occasionally, there are several fair-sized piles of soil laying on the greenish-brown grass and small patches of lawn around them that sink down when walked on. While the presence of leaves, sticks, and paper are caused by winter's gales, the mounds of dirt are the workings of moles.

Slightly larger than a mouse, moles are odd-looking creatures whose appearance nature has molded to suit their subterranean existence. Their front legs are short, yet massive compared to the rest of their body, and exceedingly powerful. Covered with a tough scale-like skin, these appendages feature long, sharp claws that allow the mole to slice through the dirt in front of it.

The thick coat of soft fur that covers its body is connected to the skin without direction. This means it can be brushed forward, backward, up, or down without resistance. Thus, the mole is able to push itself through the ground in any direction without being hindered by its fur rubbing the wrong way as it scrapes against the soil which so often engulfs it.

The head of a mole is wedge-shaped,

52

rather than rounded like that of a rodent. This allows for easier movement as it forces its way forward through the soil. Its eyes and ears are so small as to be imperceptible. This burrowing mammal seldom has the need for these sensory organs, relying almost entirely on its keen sense of smell to locate food. Like their distant relatives the shrews, moles feed mainly on invertebrate matter. Though worms seem to be particularly favored by moles, any bug or other small, squirmy organism that exists in the soil is quickly devoured.

Since rich soils seem to harbor the greatest concentration of invertebrates, moles are attracted to places with dark, loamy earth. Also, the loose, spongy nature of this type of dirt makes tunneling an easier chore. Moles will set up housekeeping immediately after finding a lawn or garden that rests upon a thick deposit of topsoil.

While moles burrowing just below the surface can cause an uneven feel to the ground, and the mounds of excavated soil can create unsightly deposits on a well-maintained lawn, their activities are helpful. Soil dwelling bugs that damage grass and other vegetation are devoured by the mole's ravenous appetite. Their tunnels allow water and air to enter the ground, benefiting the plants that grow there, and their habit of bringing dirt up to the surface is a natural form of cultivation.

Occasionally, moles are blamed for chewing on flower bulbs or destroying the roots of garden vegetables. Moles, however, do not regularly eat plant matter and are seldom responsible for this damage. Small rodents such as mice and voles often use a mole's network of tunnels in traveling about an open area in order to stay hidden from natural enemies, especially the neighborhood cat. If these tunnels enter a flower bed or a garden and pass a row of tasty bulbs or tubers, the unwelcome occupant may stay right there until the entire supply of food is exhausted.

Like most Adirondack mammals, the mole does not hibernate in winter. As frost penetrates into the ground and makes soil excavation either difficult or impossible, the mole simply works its way further downward. During years when there is only a minimal covering of snow to insulate the ground against the cold, it may have to burrow four to six feet below the surface to reach a favorable subterranean environment. Since many soil invertebrates push their way to similar depths to avoid exposure to freezing temperatures, there is usually a sufficient amount of food to keep the mole alive throughout the long winter months.

Occasionally, during winter, a mole may make its way up through its network of tunnels to forage in the caverns that exist close to the surface. There it may find dormant bugs that moved underground in the late autumn and fell into an inactive state before reaching a more suitable wintering spot.

In early April, as the frost line recedes in the Adirondacks and soil organisms begin to work their way upward, the mole also returns to life closer to the surface. This is when the mole enters into its short breeding season. After mating, the female drives off the male and begins preparing a nest for her litter in a deep underground chamber. The gestation period is believed to be about five weeks, and the young remain in their mother's care for a month or so before taking off into the soil on their own. How far maturing moles move away from their home, or at what rate they travel, is not clear.

Because they are extremely difficult to observe, not much is known about the life of this mammal. One well-documented habit of the mole is known, however. If you have a lawn in which you take great pride, or a flower bed or garden with rich, moist soil, you can expect a mole to take up residence there from mid-spring, at the start of the growing season, to late autumn, after all the yard work has been done.

The Woodcock in Spring

Bird watching is normally an activity done during the day. Except for owls and an occasional nighthawk or whippoorwill, the birds of the Adirondacks prefer the light of day to the dark of night.

During April, however, one bird causes avid ornithologists and amateur naturalists to grab a pair of binoculars and set out for a field near an alder thicket or a clearing in a damp, deciduous woodland at sunset. It is then that the woodcock, a bird that appears like an overstuffed robin with a Pinocchio condition, performs its aerial mating flight.

Known as the Timber-doodle to many a small game hunter, this bird is most active at dawn and dusk. As the sun dips below the horizon, the woodcock flies to an open field from the protective cover of a nearby patch of brush where it rested during the day. Upon arriving at a favored spot, it begins to emit a high-pitched "bzzzz" note, which it repeats every few seconds for a minute or two. It then takes to the air, climbing upward in a spiralling column, all the while making a whistling twitter sound. Just as it is nearly out of sight in the dimly lit sky, it dives earthward, gently touching down at or near the spot from which it took off. The woodcock keeps repeating this alternating process of calling and flying until the last glimmer of light disappears from the western horizon. In the twilight that precedes dawn, it will again engage in its ritual mating flight until shortly after sunrise.

The mating flight is performed only by the male and is used to advertise its presence to females that may be in the area. In the Adirondacks it ordinarily begins during the first or second week in April, shortly after the birds return from their southern wintering ground. By mid- to late May, its desire to eat during times of twilight surpasses its mating urge, and the courtship flights stop.

The woodcock is a bird that depends on earthworms as its primary source of food. Its long, hook-tipped bill is ideally adapted for catching angleworms. Scientists who have analyzed this most noticeable feature of the woodcock have discovered that it is packed with nerve endings that make it extremely sensitive to touch. This crepuscular creature is therefore able to feel the movement of worms in the soil with its bill when it is inserted into the ground. With uncanny accuracy, it pokes down in the direction of the worm to latch onto a meal.

When the woodcock arrives in the Adirondacks during early April, open fields such as golf courses, athletic fields, pasturelands, beaver meadows, and abandoned loggers staging sites may not be totally thawed. Consequently, the woodcock will concentrate much of its feeding time in those few special settings in which the ground is free of frost. Seepage areas leading into streams, partially flooded marshes, and lawns that are banked to the south are common locations visited by the woodcock upon its return.

By mid-May, most of the woodcock hens have laid their clutch of three or four eggs. A woodcock nest is located on the

55

ground, usually in a small depression behind a rock, near the base of a tree, or in the midst of a clump of brambles fifty to a hundred yards away from the male's singing field.

It takes three weeks of incubation, performed solely by the female, before the eggs hatch. Like an adult woodcock, the chicks are as difficult to see as any creature can be when on the ground. Because its mottled tan and brown plumage matches the color pattern of the dead leaves and other decaying debris of the forest floor, it is next to impossible to detect a woodcock when it is quietly sitting on the ground. The only time that the woodcock makes it presence known is during April, when the male performs his twilight aerial courtship flight.

It has been reported by naturalists that it is better to watch the woodcock's aerial display in the light of early morning rather than thirty to forty-five minutes after sunset. But the notion of getting out of a warm bed on a frosty morning before sunrise to observe a bird fly in circles may not sound appealing. It is, however, most enjoyable to be outside on a pleasant evening in mid-spring before the emergence of summer's pesky bugs to watch a woodcock. It adds significantly to the evening's delight.

The Drumming Grouse

Springtime is a season of sounds, and birds are the prime contributors to the natural music that fills the air. Throughout the Adirondack woodlands, meadows, and marshes, especially during early morning, the songs of many different birds can be heard. Over the next several weeks more summer residents will be returning from their winter ranges, and the sound will become more and more varied. Also, as the breeding season nears, the frequency and intensity of these calls will increase.

Of all these sounds, none is more distinct than that of the ruffed grouse. This chicken-like bird, also known as a partridge, does not make a vocalization. Rather, it produces a thumping noise by beating its short, powerful wings inward against its inflated chest.

The grouse begins its drumming process after ascending a fallen log from which it has a clear view of its immediate surroundings. At first, the rate at which it produces these low pitched, resonant beats is slow, about a second apart. After several beats the pace accelerates until soon they are produced in rapid succession. The sequence of thumps sounds something like a well-mufflered lawn mower starting. Approximately ten seconds after beginning, the performance abruptly ends. At this point the male fluffs his plumage, fans his tail feathers, and struts back and forth on the log. Throughout April, especially during the middle of the month, the male will repeat this act over and over again in its attempt to proclaim that particular area as its own. It is also believed that the grouse uses this sound to attract females in the area.

Unlike the whistling calls of other birds, the drumming noise of a grouse does not carry very far, especially through the dense vegetation near the forest floor. It is usually necessary to be within a hundred yards of the bird for the sound to be heard. Also, the soft nature of the noise makes it extremely difficult to determine the direction from which it is coming. Because the grouse is a ground dwelling bird it is extremely vulnerable to attack by such alert predators as the fox, coyote, bobcat, and fisher. So, when it announces its presence to other grouse, this sizeable game bird does not reveal its exact whereabouts to any of its natural enemies.

Since its call does not travel far, a male grouse often has a number of different drumming sites throughout its territory. The size of an area which a single male will claim varies depending on the availability of food. In the mixed forests of the Adirondacks, it has been estimated that one male will range over approximately seventy-five to one hundred acres. Females have been found to travel over a much greater distance and frequently stray through the territory of several males. The main activity of the cock then, during these few weeks of mid-April, is to impress any hen wandering through his territory. Hopefully, she will either stay there until the late April breeding season or return when the time comes for her to mate.

By early May most of the hens in the Adirondacks have been bred. This causes a dramatic reduction in the drumming activity of the males. Like most fowl, the male grouse parts company with the female after breeding and has nothing to do with the process of nesting or the responsibility of raising the chicks.

The grouse makes its nest on the forest floor, usually in a spot of dense underbrush, including some balsam fir, witchhobble, and maple saplings. Eight to ten brown colored eggs are laid in a shallow depression the hen fashions out of the layer of dead leaves covering the ground. Incubation lasts for three and a half weeks, so the chicks are hatching around the first or second week of June.

Ordinarily, the only occasion on which a grouse is heard, or seen for that matter, is when it flushes. As it quickly takes to the air, it makes a thunderous roar that startles most people hearing it for the first time. In April, though, it is heard in a completely different way. Listen carefully when walking through areas of dense forest cover for its low-pitched drumming call. It is unmistakable and unforgettable when heard.

Ice Out Time

There are many signs of spring. The sighting of the season's first robin, the swelling of the buds on the hardwood trees, and the reappearance of a mosquito or fly buzzing through the air all indicate that winter is behind us. But for waterfront property owners, fishermen, canoeists, and individuals who make a habit of strolling along the shore of an Adirondack lake, it is the disappearance of the ice that best indicates that spring is finally here.

Just as the opening of the lakes and ponds in the Adirondacks can help improve a person's outlook on life, so does it improve the lives of many wild creatures. As bays and coves and many miles of shoreline lose their solid winter covering, both the mink and otter greatly expand their range, and are again able to prowl the edges of lakes and ponds hunting for small animals and fish. The beaver also regains its access to the shores of the many stationary bodies of water in mid-April after being cut off from them for several months. There it will feed on the sprouting shoots of tender aquatic plants and the bark of shoreline trees and shrubs that have recently been enriched with a springtime flow of sap.

Various species of birds, whose existence is linked to large bodies of water, also begin appearing in mid-April. The osprey, a large raptor, is highly skilled at snatching fish that come to the surface to feed. Around the second week of this month, these white-bellied birds of prey begin returning to northern New York. Although the osprey does fish in flowing waterways and has been known to nest along several Adirondack rivers, it seems to prefer lakes and ponds in which to hunt for its food. If an osprey returns before the ice is out of its favorite feeding area, this impressive bird will simply fish in any open waterway that is nearby until its more traditional feeding area has thawed.

The loon, likewise, depends heavily on lake fish for its source of nourishment. This large, dark green and white bird also shows up in mid-April. Like the osprey, if the ice should linger into the latter part of this month, or even into early May, this symbol of the northern wilderness will temporarily relocate its fishing activity to a sluggish river or shallow marsh until its home body of water thaws.

The emergence of open water on the lakes is also of great benefit to those creatures that live beneath the surface, as it allows oxygen to again dissolve into the water. When covered by ice, air is unable to mix with the water, preventing oxygen from diffusing into it. Additionally, a layer of ice, especially when covered by snow, blocks sunlight from reaching the aquatic plants and algae of the lake. It is these chlorophyll-containing organisms, carrying out the oxygen-releasing process of photosynthesis, which supply a substantial amount of the oxygen to the water. As a result, from the time when the ice forms in late autumn until it thaws in spring, little oxygen is added to the lakes.

Ordinarily, enough oxygen is dissolved in the autumn to provide for the respiratory needs of the underwater inhabitants throughout the winter. Still, some aquatic organisms may perish because of the reduced oxygen concentration during early spring, particularly if cold weather persists and the ice lingers late into the month. When the ice goes out, dead fish, frogs, or insects may float to the surface or wash up on the shore. This is the time when gulls and other scavengers feast on the remains and fatten up for their approaching breeding season.

With cooperation from the weather, the ice should finally begin to disappear from the lakes and ponds over the course of the next week or two. In some places there may already be open water. While the thawing of the ice cannot come too soon for most people, the desire for open water is even stronger in many wild creatures.

Woodpecker Tapping

After observing woodpeckers, especially during the spring, it is easy to understand how these birds got their name. With their hard, durable bill, woodpeckers spend much of the time in their territory poking, probing, tapping, and pounding on branches, trunks, and almost anything else that is wooden.

For most of the year their pecking and chiseling activities are aimed solely at exposing colonies of carpenter ants, wood boring beetles, and other insects that find shelter under the bark or deep within the wood. Beginning in late winter, however, woodpeckers also rely on their pecking to produce a loud sound, called drumming, that signals the onset of their breeding season. Composed of an extremely rapid series of blows ordinarily too fast to count, this drumming lasts for only one to one and a half seconds. It may be repeated several times a minute, particularly during the early morning and an hour or two before sunset. It may also increase in frequency later in April, when the time for mating finally arrives.

A large limb that is angled upward, or the upper section of a dead trunk, are favored for drumming, as these surfaces tend to produce the loudest sounds when hit. Occasionally, woodpeckers will bang on aluminum rain gutters, metal house siding, or galvanized roofing in their attempt to locate the object that will resonate the best and carry their sound across the area.

The drumming action and its sound is entirely different from that produced when the bird is looking for food. When it searches for wood dwelling invertebrates, the woodpecker's excavating technique seldom causes a loud noise. In drumming, however, only sound is made and very little damage results to the resonant surface.

As is the case with waterfowl, the woodpeckers form a pair bond with their future mate during the late autumn. The two birds, however, have very little to do with one another throughout the winter since they must concentrate all of their energy on obtaining food. But as the days lengthen and more time becomes available to them, these birds begin to turn their attention towards mating. Re-establishing this pair bond is their first concern, and drumming is their means of locating one another in the forest.

Some researchers also believe drumming serves as a warning to their woodpecker neighbors that trespassing into the area will not be tolerated. Later in the month, drumming is thought to be used by both male and female to lead their mate to potential nesting sites. Although some individuals may reuse their nesting cavity from the previous year, most end up excavating a new hole each spring.

Because of its size, the pileated, or red-crested, woodpecker must select a trunk that will provide an appropriately large chamber. Roughly the size of a crow, this woodpecker digs out a hole that averages nine inches across and about one and a half feet deep. The hairy and downy woodpeckers, along with the flicker and sapsucker, are known to make their nests in either a limb or trunk of nearly any type of tree. While a piece of dead timber is usually chosen, live aspens may also be used because of their relatively soft wood.

On occasion a pair bond may abandon one site after beginning the task of excavation in favor of another spot. What may have first appeared to the woodpeckers to be the perfect tree for a nest probably turned out to be either too hard or too soft and unstable. Also, a previously unnoticed neighbor, such as a red squirrel, may cause the pair to relocate to another site.

Work on the nest takes place sporadically throughout the day and may take as long as two weeks to complete. Although both the male and female work on the cavity, it is the male that does the majority of the work. Some naturalists theorize that this allows the female to conserve her energy at a time when nutrients for egg formation are needed.

The presence of wood chips freshly scattered around the base of a tree during mid- to late April may indicate the location of a woodpecker nesting cavity. The tree containing the nest will show only a rounded hole that serves as the entrance to the chamber. Foraging activities also leave pieces of wood on the ground. However, this type of excavation usually results in trees with large gashes in the bark or one to several sizeable holes in the wood.

After the eggs are laid, woodpeckers continue to drum, although not at the same intensity as during April and early May. By mid-summer, drumming becomes infrequent, and by September their urge to rapidly rap their bill on a resonant surface fades altogether.

Like other birds, woodpeckers produce a variety of other sounds. Each species has its own repertoire of vocalizations that are said to serve very specific purposes. Overall, though, these birds are best known for the drumming sound, which also helps characterize this sound-filled season.

The Ruler of the Shoreline

The feature that many people know about the mink is that it bears a dark brown, soft fur which is extremely valuable in coats, stoles, collars, and other articles of high-priced outer clothing. Yet, the wild mink is also a common and important resident of the many marshes, rivers, streams, and lakeshores of the Adirondacks.

Unlike its close relative the otter, which spends much of its time in the water, the mink is a shoreline creature, and the more intricate the nature of the shore, the more likely that mink will occur there in greater numbers. Aquatic settings in which there are numerous points of dry land jutting out into the open water, and frequent mounds of woody plants and dead vegetation forming small, offshore islands, are ideal for the mink. Places in which the water's edge is littered with partially submerged logs and stumps, or where piles of boulders form small cubbies and hidden passageways, are also highly attractive to this sleek member of the weasel family.

The presence of shoreline irregularities provide the mink with both a choice of housing and an increased opportunity for ambushing prey. Unlike most other animals, the mink often maintains up to a dozen different denning sites. As it travels about its territory, it is likely to stop and rest or eat a recently caught meal in the confines of one of its often grass-lined shelters. These can be in almost any natural protective enclosure that exists near

62

the water's edge. Mink are also known to temporarily take up residence in abandoned beaver lodges and muskrat huts or burrows.

This habit of using one spot for only a limited period of time helps prevent fleas, lice, and other skin parasites from becoming too numerous in its bedding material. Should a mink vacate a den for several weeks, these tiny, irritating invertebrates either die or relocate to a more favorable place.

Beginning in mid- to late April, the female mink concentrates most of her time around a single den, where she will bear her annual litter of from two to nine offspring. Known as kits, young mink are small at birth and develop slowly compared to the young of some other mammals. It takes from four to five weeks for their eyes to open, and they are not likely to leave the safety of their den until they are at least a month and a half old.

Because of their delicate nature, the mother doesn't leave them for very long when she goes out in search of food for herself. Though in winter prey is scarce, by mid-April hunting conditions change dramatically. Shortly after the ice goes out and the water begins to warm, the breeding season of frogs, toads, and salamanders approaches and they start populating the shore. The still cold temperature of the water, however, reduces the reaction time of these cold-blooded amphibians, making them easy marks for the agile mink.

Also in late April, some species of fish spend much of their time near the shore. Because of the slightly warmer water in the shallows, and the greater abundance of food there during mid-spring, fish become plentiful in places that are within the mink's reach.

Late April is also the time when most Adirondack waterfowl nest. Occasionally a mink is able to sneak up on a duck that is sitting on her clutch of eggs. If this predator fails to snag the hen, it still gets to feast on her highly nutritious eggs.

The abundance of food in aquatic areas from late April until early June allows the female to remain within several hundred yards of the natal den. As a rule, female mink tend to travel much less than males. Even in winter, the female will often restrict her movements to an area of only fifty to sixty acres. The territory of a male is many times that of the female, and they have been known to range well over several miles from a central point.

The larger territory of the male often encompasses the home range of several females. During the late winter breeding season, one male usually services all of those females within the boundaries of his domain.

The role of the male in the rearing of the young varies. In some cases, naturalists have reported that the male mink does play some role in raising its offspring. However, there are also many cases in which the female was observed to be the sole caretaker.

From time to time, fishermen, canoeists, and homeowners with a view of the water's edge may notice a rather lanky, dark brown animal with short legs sneaking about the shore. This is a mink, and if seen repeatedly in the same area, the chances are that its newborn family is close by.

Two Adirondack Amphibians

Toward the end of April, it seems that every day adds a new sound to the many natural noises that already fill the air. While most of these sounds are made by birds, a few are produced by amphibians.

In the Adirondacks, the wood frog is normally the first of these moist-skinned creatures to begin its mating serenade. Shortly after the ground thaws in mid-April, the wood frog emerges from its state of hibernation and immediately heads to the closest pool of water on the forest floor. Unlike other frogs that spend the winter under water, this small brown creature with its black mask spends the winter burrowed underground. Any place where the soil is loose and easy to work its way into will attract the wood frog.

Large puddles created by melting snow and spring rains that remain intact for several months are the traditional sites used by the wood frog for breeding. Soon after arriving at these seasonal bodies of water, the wood frog begins producing a series of slow, clacking sounds. From a distance, this call resembles the noise of a nervous duck quacking in slow motion.

For the wood frog, the breeding season seldom lasts longer than a week or two. After mating is completed, this shy creature begins its journey back to some favored spot amidst the moist leaf litter deep in the forest. Approximately six weeks after they are laid, the jelly-like eggs hatch into tiny tad- poles. These re-

64

main in the woodland pools until the water dries up at the start of summer.

While the sound of the wood frog lasts for only a brief time, the mating call of the spring peeper can be heard for most of the spring. Beginning in late April, about two weeks after the ice goes out, until mid-June, this tiny amphibian, which is classified as a tree frog, announces its presence with a series of loud "peeps." Along the shore of alder brooks, near the edge of weedy marshes, and in flooded fields, the spring peeper numbers in the hundreds and thousands. The resulting chorus produced by the multitude can be awe inspiring, especially on a pleasant evening after a warm spring rain. Because it is cold-blooded, the spring peeper's rate of activity is directly related to the temperature of its surroundings. During mild periods, the volume and intensity of the peeper's mating serenade increases noticeably. During the late afternoon and throughout the evening, the chorus is loud enough to make it impossible to home in on any one particular caller, even if it is directly beneath your feet.

On the other hand, frosty evenings cause the peepers to become sluggish. While some do not utter their single-note call at all, others sound off only a few times every minute. On these chilly occasions, it is possible to identify the exact spot from which a peeper is singing, though actually seeing one is exceptionally difficult. The spring peeper averages only an inch in length and is the exact same color as that of its background. Additionally, when it is calling, the peeper may be partially immersed in water or surrounded by a veil of grassy shoots or a curtain of leaves, making it next to impossible to see.

Like all other tailless amphibians, only the male spring peeper sings. Also, at this time of year, the male is said to be slightly darker than the female. Consequently, should you happen to notice two that are together, odds are that the darker one is the male.

Like the wood frog, the spring peeper spends the winter underground burrowed beneath the frost line. As soon as the soil thaws, it pushes its way to the surface and heads toward the nearest pond, marsh, or aldered brook. Its tolerance for near-freezing temperatures makes it one of the first amphibians to awaken in the spring. That toughness also makes the spring peeper ideally suited to the climate of the northern mountains.

The air in the Adirondacks during mid-spring always seems to be especially fragrant and full of sounds. While many of the noises of this season are pleasant to listen to, none is as spellbinding as the chorus of the nearly invisible tree frogs.

The Bumble Bee

Because of the frequent cold spells and the limited supply of food at the end of April and early May, most insects do not emerge from their winter dormancy until the middle part of May. There are, however, some bugs that may be seen out and about before the lawns turn green and yellow dandelion heads begin to sprout. Species of spiders, caterpillars, beetles, and flies begin appearing as soon as the surface of the ground thaws.

The bumble bee is one of those hardy insects that may be noted early in the season. The larger size of this bee, compared to its other stinging relatives, allows it to conserve body heat more effectively, as does its thicker coat of black and yellow hair. Other internal features also adapt it to the cold, thereby allowing it to be active during times when other bees aren't. On cool days in late May and early June, when there is a biting north wind, or during the later evening hours or very early morning when chilly temperatures cause other bees to retreat into temporary shelter, the bumble bee may be noticed visiting shivering blossoms or dew-covered flowers.

Unlike other bugs, the bumble bee does not experience the form of winter dormancy known as diapause. Like many other early risers, it spends the winter in a state of torpor, and awakens in response to favorable temperatures.

To insure that they will not emerge prematurely during a mid-winter thaw, bumble bees usually winter in the ground on the north slope of a hill, or in a sun-sheltered ravine. In these protected locations, spring is slow in coming. By the time the snow finally disappears and the ground thaws, triggering their awakening, chances are that conditions for their survival are good.

Should a cold snap send the mercury plummeting, or a snowfall again blanket the ground, as can often happen at this time of year, the bumble bee simply burrows into the leaf litter that covers the soil, or retreats into some other sheltered spot and becomes dormant until the weather improves.

As is the case with wasps, the only individuals that survive the winter are the fertile females, known as queens, which have mated the previous autumn with a drone. An abandoned mouse or vole nest is reported to be the favored wintering site of the bumble bee. An unused section of a mole tunnel, or an unoccupied subterranean chamber of a chipmunk or woodchuck, are other places in which the bumble bee is known to pass the winter.

While a hole in the ground may serve as a hibernating spot, such a site may not be suitable as a place for a colony. Therefore, the first order of business for an awakened bumble bee queen is to find a location in which she can establish her breeding nest. This is why bumble bees may be seen at this time of year exploring nooks and crannies, such as openings in the eaves of houses, large cracks in masonry walls, or small cavities in partially rotted trees.

Construction of a cell in which approximately a dozen eggs will be placed is the next chore confronting the queen once she has decided on a particular spot for her nest. (A bumble bee constructs a nest while a honey bee builds a hive.) The collection of nectar and pollen then begins, with the food stored in a crude container near the egg cell. When the eggs hatch into larvae, the immature bees require more food per day than the queen can gather. She will then feed them from the limited reserve previously collected.

Approximately five to six weeks after the eggs are laid, adult bumble bees emerge from the cell. These are all workers and immediately begin helping the queen with the many chores around the nest. Additional eggs are laid for the second, third, and fourth rank of workers that will help the first. By mid-summer, there may be a hundred or more adult bees in the colony.

Like other bees, the bumble bee is capable of inflicting a painful sting if it is disturbed. However, like the honey bee, this large, rather slow flying insect is extremely beneficial to the environment and should not be killed simply because a person is afraid of it. Bumble bees are important in the pollination process, helping to ensure that fruit will form on a plant. Bumble bees are especially valuable during years when unseasonably cold weather dominates the Adirondacks during the late spring. If the temperature is too cold for honey bees to pollinate plants, it is the bumble bees that take over this important function.

MAY

Woodland Wildflowers

Throughout Adirondack meadows and along roadsides, the peak of the flowering season extends from mid-June through very early August. However, in the vast expanse of forests that covers so much of the region, only the month of May is known for its wildflowers.

Because of their sensitivity to frost, most plants that grow in open areas are slow to sprout in spring. It is not until the time that students are finishing the school year that the first of nature's series of colorful floral displays blossom in undisturbed sunlit settings.

The process of flowering requires a great deal of energy and the only source of energy in green plants is the sun. This is why a sun-bathed meadow is able to support such a tremendous abundance and diversity of wildflowers. While various species are able to survive in shade by absorbing reflected and diffused light, even these plants need the direct rays of the sun to carry out the functions required to blossom.

In heavily wooded areas, the lack of direct sunlight reaching the ground during summer severely inhibits the formation of flowers on a plant. It is only from the last few days of April, until the leaves erupt from their buds and the canopy closes overhead, that there is adequate sunlight for blossoming in most of the region's woodland wildflowers. As a result, the peak of the flowering season across the Adirondacks begins now and continues for the next several weeks to a month.

The first plants to appear are the spring beauty and trout lily, also known as dog tooth violet. Both have roots saturated with the nutrients needed for rapid development. Because of their food value, Native Americans once collected these tiny tubers, though their small size made it difficult to gather enough for a filling meal. But, for mice, jumping mice, and voles, only a handful of these bulbs can provide enough nourishment for several days. When their leaves sprout, usually as soon as the snow melts, deer also nibble on them, finding them an especially tasty treat after five months spent gnawing only on the buds of trees.

Trillium, better known to some people as stinkpot, is the next plant to sprout and bloom in spring. This attractive wildflower, in its various forms, relies on carrion-eating insects for pollination. At this time of year, many of the insects that are attracted to flower nectar are not yet active. However, bugs that feed on dead animal matter, particularly on the remains of the creatures that were unable to survive the winter, are usually quick to emerge from their period of dormancy. In producing a smell that resembles the odor of decaying flesh, trillium is able to successfully lure these insects to it.

Yellow and purple violets, jack-in-the-pulpit, and miterwort are plants that will also be supporting delicate petaled flowers in Adirondack hardwood forests over the course of the next several weeks.

In evergreen woodlands the flower season begins slightly later, occurring from mid-May to the first week of June. While some shade is always present in dense stands of conifers, the amount of light reaching the ground dwindles considerably following Memorial Day. While evergreens possess a substantial covering of needles throughout the year, these trees sprout additional layers of foliage in early June. This thickens the canopy, further limiting the amount of sun striking the ground. Consequently, for the plants that flourish in the carpet of dead needles, flowering must be accomplished by mid-June.

Bunchberry, wild lily-of-the-valley, bluebead lily, maystar, goldthread, and lady slippers are a common part of the evergreen forests of the Adirondacks that will be in bloom by the end of this month.

When dandelions are beginning to bear their yellow reproductive structures in fields and lawns, the list of wildflowers that are ready to bloom in these woodlands is as extensive as the petals of the plants are delicate. The presence of such scattered clumps of plants, along with the music of the resident birds, the fresh smell of the forest air, and the absence of pesky insects (at least for another few weeks), all combine to make a walk through an Adirondack woodland during the first half of this month a more pleasurable experience than at any other time of the year.

The Song of the White-Throated Sparrow

There are many bird songs that are familiar to Adirondack residents. The wailing cry of the loon and the hooting of an owl are easily recognizable sounds. The cheerful chirping of a robin, the boisterous squawking of the blue jay, and the noisy cawing of a crow are calls learned early in life and are as natural a part of the environment as the mountains and trees. None of these calls, however, is as distinct and characteristic of the Adirondacks as the melodious song of the white-throated sparrow.

Beginning with its arrival during the latter half of April, and continuing through the summer, this small handsome sparrow announces its presence by reciting its unique eleven-note song. The first two notes of its call differ in pitch and are of a longer duration than the rest. (Generally the second note is higher in pitch than the first, although it may be sung lower on some occasions.) The remaining notes follow quickly in three series of three notes each, all of which are the same pitch. The expression "Old Sam Peabody-Peabody-Peabody" has been used for generations to describe this simple, yet conspicuous song.

Like the call of most other birds, this tune is repeatedly sung early in the morning, especially at sunrise, when the air is alive with springtime sounds. It may also be commonly heard on warm days when the air is moist and fragrant and the winds are calm. Evening is another time when the white-throated sparrow spends much of its time singing, often to the accompaniment of the flute-like song of the hermit thrush and the whistling melody of the robin.

Unlike any other perching bird, the white-throated sparrow will occasionally sing at night. As it enters its breeding season around the first week of May, and continuing on through June, this bird seems to suffer from bouts of insomnia. Throughout the night, a lone call may be heard coming from one location or another every ten to twenty minutes. This nocturnal singing habit may be readily noticed at this time of the year when sitting outside on a deck or porch long after the sun has set, or when the weather permits a bedroom window to be left open all night.

Although its song can be heard in many different settings throughout the Adirondacks, it is far more common in semi-open areas in which there is both dense underbrush and an abundance of evergreen trees. The white-throated sparrow is a ground-dwelling creature and prefers to nest and forage for food on or near the forest floor. Because life on the ground makes it so vulnerable to attack by predators, this small bird prefers to reside in places in which its activities are well concealed from view. The shores of lakes, the edges of small woodland clearings, and overgrown fields are all settings attractive to it because of the very dense layer of undergrowth at these sites.

Upper elevation forests and the summits of the High Peaks also serve as breeding sites for the white-throated sparrow. Although the weather on high mountain slopes may be less than desirable to people, this small bird does not seem to mind such harsh conditions. The impenetrable stands of dwarf conifers and dense clumps of cold, hardy shrubs that characterize these arctic-like areas provide a favorable setting for this sparrow to live.

Because it prefers a life among tangled clusters of small shrubs, tall ferns, weeds, grasses, and dead conifer limbs, this sparrow, with the small white patch on its throat and yellow spot between its eye and bill, is not an easy bird to see. Glimpses of it can be caught from time to time as it

71

hops about the maze of material on the forest floor. It may also be seen when it scratches the surface of the ground in its attempt to uncover food. During dry weather, when the layer of dead leaves that blankets the soil is exceptionally crisp, it may also be noticed as it forcefully flings its feet backwards, making a noticeable rustling sound.

The fallen seeds of evergreens form a substantial portion of its diet, as do the tiny seed from weeds, forest wildflowers, shrubs, and various hardwood trees. Insects are also eaten if they are uncovered and caught before they dart beneath the dead leaves again.

While you are out working in the yard, getting the garden ready, sitting on the porch, or in a boat, there are many sounds that can be heard. Some of them are the soft calls of unfamiliar birds which may be hard to hear, while others are the sounds of well-known birds that can be heard almost anytime of the year. And then there is the sound of the white-throated sparrow, which means that spring has come to the Adirondacks and summer is not too far away.

The Beneficial Earthworm

In the Adirondacks, May is the time of year for working in the soil. This is particularly true of the first half of the month, before swarms of black flies make outside activities difficult, if not impossible. Any chore, however, that disturbs the soil, like tilling the garden, digging in a flower bed, or planting trees, exposes some of the many tiny creatures which reside in this uppermost layer of earth. Large white grubs are occasionally noticed, along with their adult form, the June Bug, which begins to stir from its winter dormancy as the soil warms in May. The rounded body of a millipede or the flat-shaped centipede may be uncovered when a clump of dirt near the surface is overturned. None of these animals, however, is as numerous or has such a significant impact on the health and well-being of the soil as the earthworm.

Earthworms are creatures that occur in places where the soil is rich and moist. During the day they remain several inches below ground, while at night they push their way up to the surface to search for small pieces of decomposing matter. Fallen leaves of aspens, birch, and ash are especially favored by these squirmy creatures, while those of the maples are taken only if little else is available. The leaves of beech and the needles of most conifers seem to be avoided, regardless of their abundance. Seeds, the blades of dead grasses, the rotting stems of certain weeds, and other types of decomposing matter may also be eaten.

Because they are so highly prized as food to so many ground dwelling creatures, worms spend as little time on the surface as possible. Once they have stumbled upon something that meets their taste, they quickly pull themselves into the entrance of their burrow to consume it, rather than devour it on the surface. In addition, while they are searching for food, earthworms keep a portion of their rear end in their burrow. Thus, should a predator, such as an angler looking for bait, grab onto one, the worm has a fighting chance at pulling free and quickly retreating beneath the soil's surface. Worms have four sets of short bristles on each of their many body segments that can firmly grab onto the walls of their burrows. Considerable force must often be exerted on them in order to extract them from their hole after grabbing onto their front end. (The front end of a worm can be determined by the presence of the *clitellum*, a noticeably swollen section of their body roughly one-fourth of the way back from their mouth.)

In places where the ground has been cleared of most dead matter, such as on a well-raked lawn, worms are forced to swallow the soil in an attempt to absorb the dead matter it contains. When they come to the surface at night, they then deposit this soil, minus its nutrients, in a small pile over the entrance of their burrow. These clumps of soil, along with their own wastes, are known as castings.

Castings are seen in places where the ground is fairly hard packed. In areas with loose dirt, worms are able to simply push their way between soil particles as they move up and down in their subterranean world. In settings where the ground is more compact, earthworms must swallow the soil in order to move through it. In this way a worm literally eats its way up to the surface.

The miniature passageways which these tunneling creatures create in the soil are helpful in allowing air to permeate to lower depths. They also increase the ability of water to percolate down, especially after periods of heavy rain. Since both of these substances are of vital importance to the roots of plants, vegetation usually grows well in areas where earthworms are abundant.

In the Adirondacks there are two main types of worms: the large and fairly robust night crawler and the smaller angle worm. While both may live in the same area, night crawlers construct better burrows and tend to travel deeper into the soil. During the winter, they may descend six feet or more below the surface. Angle worms, however, spend more of their time closer to the surface, and do not have as elaborate or well-defined burrows as the night crawler.

Despite a popular belief to the contrary, soil is not just dirt. It is a complex mixture of various particles and minerals, along with the decomposing remains of organisms that have long since died. Within this material there exists a wealth of living matter, both plant and animal. All have their own special roles to play in this darkened environment, yet none seems to be as important as the earthworm.

Time for a Hummingbird Feeder

Maintaining a bird feeder next to a window in your home can provide a close-up view of a variety of birds and allow for some interesting wildlife observations. Not all feeders, however, need to be an open-ended container stocked with sunflower seeds or wild bird food. From the time the apple blossoms first open in mid-May, until the yellowish stalks of goldenrod finally fade around Labor Day, the hummingbird may be lured to a patio, deck, or window with a sweetened watery solution.

Like the honeybee, the hummingbird feeds on the nectar secreted by various flowers, pollinating the flower in the process. Its long, needle-like bill enables it to reach into the heart of tubular flowers, such as the beebalm, cardinal flower, and petunia. At this time of year apple blossoms serve as a source of food, as does honeysuckle. The hummingbird is also equipped with a tongue that is adapted for lapping up every drop of sweetened fluid that forms at the base of these attractive flowers.

A liquid solution composed of four parts water and one part table sugar works effectively as a substitute for flower nectar. Such a mixture should be placed in a small container that is either bright red or orange, or has a similarly colored top. Flowers that secrete nectar advertise the fact by producing colorful petals. It is the color, more than an attractive aroma, that lures this tiny bird to investigate the blossoms of a plant, or in this case, a hummingbird feeder. It is interesting to note that color is also more attractive than shape, as a hummingbird will check out any and all brightly colored objects regardless of their design.

These feeders should always be equipped with a lid or be of such design as to minimize evaporation. During spells of hot, dry weather the water can quickly disappear into the atmosphere. A lid or a container sealed at the top also prevents the contents from becoming overly diluted with water during periods of heavy rain. Only a small hole is needed for this bird to get its bill into the water inside.

People who mix up their own sugar water for their hummingbird feeders should be aware that these solutions can ferment or become contaminated with harmful bacteria in a short span of time. During periods of exceptionally warm weather, and especially if it is located in the sun, the container should be cleaned out every other day and restocked with a fresh solution. During cool weather, or if the feeder is located in a shady spot, changing the syrupy contents may be necessary only once a week. Mixtures can be purchased in stores that contain the needed preservatives to prevent fermentation or spoilage from occurring.

Along with their frequent trips to such feeders, hummingbirds also consume a large number of bugs. Under natural conditions, these birds first gulp down the small insects that have entered the flower looking for a meal of sweets. It has been estimated by some researchers that the diet of a hummingbird is about fifty percent bugs and fifty percent nectar. A visitor at a feeder may be seen attempting to lap up some bug that had found its way into the container and drowned in the syrupy trap.

Observing the hummingbird away from a feeder is not an easy task. Because of its small size, nearly invisible wing beats, and rapid rate of flight, the hummingbird is one of the most challenging birds to follow. It often lights on a twig near a feeder to rest between its short meals and may be watched or photographed there. However, once it has satisfied its appetite for sweets, the hummingbird quickly disappears into the surroundings.

Over the course of the next two weeks, the hummingbird will be returning to the Adirondacks from its wintering grounds in the tropics of South America. Since the region occasionally experiences a cold snap or two before summer finally arrives, making natural food sources temporarily scarce, a feeder will act like an oasis in the desert until the flowers open again.

Because hummingbirds in the Adirondacks concentrate much of their time around feeders during cold periods, activities other than feeding may be observed on these occasions. The male, which is identified by the greater amount of iridescence, does not waste much time after returning before beginning to perform his courtship ritual in front of the female.

Nesting occurs in June, and it is a most fortunate person that happens to locate a hummingbird nest. Because of its extremely small size (roughly that of a walnut shell), the bird's knack for building it in an area of dense brush, and the protective coloration of the mother, finding a hummingbird nest is accomplished only by chance. Such secretive nesting instincts stand in sharp contrast to their often bold attempts to collect sugar water from a porch, deck, lawn, or window sill.

It's Blackfly Time

As the deciduous woodlands of the Adirondacks turn green with the emergence of leaves, thin, evasive clouds of tiny black insects begin to appear. Beginning in mid-May and continuing through Memorial Day, the population of adult blackflies explodes. Swarms of these noxious bugs hover around your head, light on your neck and eyelids, fly into your ears, and crawl over your scalp. They can be inhaled, making you choke, and they bite, causing you to bleed. Some people are allergic to the saliva-like fluid which they secrete into the skin upon piercing it, and often experience more discomfort as the bites swell, inflaming that area of the body.

Blackflies compose a group of insects that are properly known as Buffalo Gnats. This label has been applied to them by scientists because of their humped back, which resembles that of the American bison. In the Adirondacks, there are over a dozen different species of these prolific bugs, although only six or seven types find humans to their liking. Most blackflies prefer the host of other warm-blooded creatures that populate the woodlands, especially those that live near the forest floor.

Like mosquitoes, it is the female blackfly that has mated that is looking for a meal of blood. She needs certain animal proteins contained in blood that provide nutrients vital for proper egg development. The males and unmated females are concerned only with finding each other to breed and so do not bother humans or other animals.

Once she has mated and obtained her fill of blood, the female then attempts to locate a stream, brook, or other flowing body of water in which to deposit her eggs. Unlike mosquitoes, which spend their larval stage in stagnant water, blackflies require flowing water in which to develop into adults. The more mountainous a region or the steeper the terrain, the faster the water moves in the brooks, rivers, and streams that flow through these areas. This is one of the reasons why these pesky bugs are more abundant in the mountains than in the lowland regions.

Also, during this larval stage, blackflies cannot tolerate warm water. In some cases, water temperatures of only 60° can be lethal, which is why these bugs are more likely to be encountered in northern settings rather than in milder climatic areas.

The microscopically small eggs of the blackfly are laid in a single-layered cluster which often contains over a hundred future insects. This cluster is usually placed on a rock, log, stick, leaf, or some other object that juts just above the surface of the rushing water. Occasionally the eggs are washed into the current and eventually settle to the bottom where they become lodged against some stone, piece of wood, or particles of gravel.

After hatching, the tiny, caterpillar-like larvae attach themselves to that object and gradually move up it, so as to be in the current as much as possible. During this stage of their life, blackflies feed on microorganisms which they filter from the water flowing past them.

After passing through a half dozen larval stages, these immature insects enter the pupa stage. Like many other bugs, blackflies cover themselves with a silk-like material to form a cocoon while they transform into adults. When the metamorphic change is completed, the adult rips it away and rises to the surface, usually inside a tiny bubble of air.

Despite the persistent attacks that plague people and wildlife, black-flies have their place in nature. During the mid- to late spring, when they are most abundant, they serve as an important source of food to many animals, especially birds, which, as they prepare to lay their eggs and raise their brood, require a greater amount of protein than at other times of the year. While they certainly rank as one of the most despised of all insects, their presence marks the official beginning of the second and best half of spring in the Adirondacks.

Keep Your Eyes Open for Loons

Along with the massive swarms of blackflies, there are many other forms of insect life that hatch in great numbers in mid-May. The increase in insect activity, along with the warming of the water in the lakes and ponds, triggers the urge in experienced trout anglers to abandon all else, pack up the canoe and fishing tackle, and head out to some remote pond.

It is in these traditional trout waters that the loon, one of the symbols of the Great North Woods, is encountered. A few days after the ice goes out in mid-April, the loon returns from its wintering areas off the mid-Atlantic coast. If the bird arrives before the ice has left, it cannot gain access to its home body of water. When this happens, the loon will simply wait in a river or attempt to find open water in a sheltered, sunny bay or cove until the ice on the lake disappears.

Despite the hypothermic condition of the water, the loon will spend all of its time either swimming on the surface or diving for food. A special layer of fat on its underside, along with an exceptionally dense covering of plumage, help to insulate this large northern bird from the cold. Also, like other aquatic animals, the loon keeps its feathers well pruned with a water repellent oil that keeps it dry.

It is not long after their return that a

lake's resident pair of loons will re-establish the bond between them. Many naturalists believe that these primitive birds mate for life and return to the same body of water they claimed the previous year. Following a brief court-ship period, the pair begins the process of constructing a nest. Floating sticks, water logged twigs, and assorted aquatic grass and weed stems are collected and assembled into a circular mound that is usually placed di-rectly along the water's edge. Because the loon's legs are located so near its tail, an adaptation that allows for an incredible degree of maneuverabil-ity in the water, it finds it nearly impossible to walk on land. As a result, the loon always erects its nest in a spot that it can simply swim directly to and flop inside.

In order to prevent the nest from being destroyed by large waves, the loon always selects a sheltered cove or bay in which to place it. Leeward sides of small islands are especially favored as nesting sites because they offer protection from waves and have few predators prowling the shores. A mink or an otter may be the only threat in such a location, because rac-coons, foxes, coyotes, bobcats, and other land dwelling creatures would be unlikely to plunder its nest on such shores.

Over the past half century, one of the greatest dangers facing this im-pressive bird has been the presence of motor boat traffic near its nest. A large speedboat creates a substantial wake, even if it is not traveling very fast. A small wave can destroy the eggs in the nest by crashing over the low rim of this delicate platform.

Another threat that humans pose to breeding loons is their presence too close to the nest. Because of its wary nature, a loon incubating its eggs will leave its nest whenever a person gets close in a canoe, guideboat, or small power craft. Instinctively, the parent tries to lead the intruder away from the site by performing a strange surface display. First, it rears up on its legs, almost as if it were standing on its tail, then flops over and over in the water, emitting the haunting cry for which it is so well-known.

The longer people sit and marvel at this awe-inspiring performance, the longer the eggs are exposed to the cool air, endangering their chances for successful hatching. Occasionally anglers will unknowingly keep a loon off its nest by drifting too near, concentrating more on casting a fly for a rising trout than on a display they may have seen before.

The loon lays its two eggs immediately after completing the nest, which in the Adirondacks is some time in mid-May, and then begins the four week process of incubation. It is just before school gets out for the year and the flood of summer visitors arrives that its chicks hatch and the loon abandons its nest for a life in the water. When the infant birds want to rest, they simply climb up on their mother's back and nestle in the hollow between her wings and neck.

It may seem an incredible chore to haul a canoe into some remote pond or lake during the spring simply to catch fish. However, there are rewards other than a frying pan full of brook trout. There is also the immeasurable pleasure of listening to the cry of the loon.

The Blossoming of the Alpine Wildflowers

For many tourist-related businesses, Memorial Day weekend marks the start of the summer season. This weekend also marks the beginning of the growing season atop the Adirondacks' tallest mountain peaks. During this time, the snow finally starts to disappear on the summits and warmer weather becomes the rule rather than the exception. It is also the time when small ground plants that cover these treeless slopes spring to life after being dormant for nearly nine months. During the next several weeks, these hardy species of arctic and alpine plants form seeds and produce a store of nutrients in preparation for winter's return. The absence of trees at these high altitudes is the result of the severe cold, the wind's strength, and the winter air. Only plants lying close to the ground are able to survive in this hostile environment. Even during the summer, growing con-

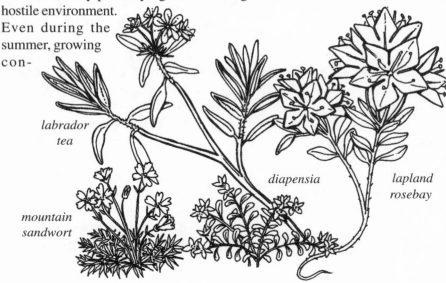

labrador
tea

mountain
sandwort

diapensia

lapland
rosebay

ditions are less than ideal. The combination of intense sunlight in the thin air and strong winds draws moisture from both plants and soil, creating a desert-like dryness.

However, as any experienced High Peaks hiker knows, conditions on these summits can quickly and dramatically change. Summer drought conditions can give way to clouds and heavy showers that pelt the unprotected slopes. The pitch of the terrain causes most of this water to run off, and the soil's shallow depth, coupled with the extreme rate of evaporation, causes a speedy return to arid conditions. Adding to this drastic, climatic see-saw is the midsummer frost that can strike at the highest altitudes on clear nights when the air is calm.

Despite such unfavorable growing conditions, there are plants that are well suited for life above the timberline. They can tolerate weather that would quickly kill other plants and are able to compress their active life into the few short months that the temperature remains above freezing. Flowering is usually their first order of business. Their delicate blossoms start to appear shortly after the snow melts, and in some cases even before the soil is completely thawed.

In late May and early June clumps of white flowered diapensia can be seen hugging rock surfaces. These are sometimes found alongside tiny mats of pink colored alpine azaleas. Small clusters of bright pink lapland rosebay adorn windswept slopes, and the delicate, white-petaled mountain sandwort takes root in the soil in small cracks and shallow depressions. Three-toothed cinque-foil and labrador tea also add color to this already spectacular vista.

As delicate as these flowers are, the overall nature of this setting is even more fragile. The soil of the Adirondack peaks is very shallow and extremely sensitive to the trampling action of hikers boots. Vibrum soles especially tend to loosen the tiny layer of peat moss and dirt in which these plants grow. These disturbed patches can quickly wash away when exposed to the eroding effects of the wind and rain. To prevent this destruction, hikers are strongly encouraged to stay on the designated trails and avoid walking across these alpine meadows.

The scenic view from atop Mt. Marcy, Algonquin, Haystack, and Skylight is nothing short of magnificent. Over the next few weeks, the spectacular panorama will become a landscape dotted with clusters and clumps of attractive wildflowers. If you plan on venturing up any of these four peaks, be aware that the weather can quickly revert to arctic conditions.

Also be careful to walk only on the trails, as an innocent stroll over the fragile vegetation can cause harm to this environment that may take years to restore.

Turtles Begin Laying Eggs

During the last few days of May, turtles in the Adirondack lakes begin to leave their aquatic environment. Around Memorial Day weekend, these ancient vertebrates leave the murky, watery depths they prefer to inhabit in order to lay their eggs on dry land.

After mating, which can occur several weeks to a month prior to egg laying, the female turtle journeys to an open area where the soil is suitable for digging. The edge of a seldom used dirt road or the tracks of an abandoned railroad line are frequently selected sites, as are sandy banks near the shore where there are few trees overhead.

Because reptiles, being cold-blooded, do not incubate their eggs, they must rely on outside sources of warmth to nurture the embryo inside. For turtles, this means open areas where their buried eggs are exposed to the rays of the summer sun.

Once an appropriate spot has been found, the turtle begins the laborious chore of excavating a hole. The digging begins with its front legs, then shifts to its hind legs after only a few scoops of dirt are removed. Its long and sharp claws enable it to scratch through hard-packed soil without too much difficulty. The final depth of the hole equals the distance of its outstretched hind legs.

There are two common species of turtles in the Adirondacks. The painted turtle, the smaller of the two, ordinarily carves out a hole about four inches deep. The snapping turtle, well known for its size and unpleasant disposition, can dig a hole over half a foot in depth.

Once egg laying begins, little interrupts the process. Forty to fifty soft, rubbery, white eggs are deposited in the hole before they are covered. The eggs of the snapping turtle look very much like ping-pong balls, spherical and nearly the same size.

Unlike bird eggs, the eggs of turtles are encased in a flexible, leathery shell. This soft covering allows moisture to penetrate inside and provides for the exchange of gases.

Because of their rich nutrient content, turtle eggs are prized by many creatures. Raccoons, foxes, coyotes, skunks, bears, weasels, and mink are but a few of the many wild creatures that enjoy unearthing a cluster of them, especially after they have just been laid. It's not unusual to notice a scattered pile of torn shells next to a hole in the soil during this time of year.

The eggs that are not discovered by a predator often remain in the ground for most of the summer. Because of the limited amount of warmth in the Adirondacks, development of the embryo is slow, and occasionally the eggs of snapping turtles may not hatch until autumn. Such hatchlings often remain buried until the soil thaws the following spring.

Adirondack turtles are thought to be totally aquatic creatures. During the late spring, however, a lone turtle can be encountered groping through an open field or slowly crossing a highway. Don't be too concerned about getting it back into a nearby marsh or pond, as most likely it is searching for a spot in which to bury its eggs.

JUNE

The Adirondacks' Number One Bird

The Adirondack landscape is composed of many different ecological settings, each with its own outstanding resident bird. In marshlands, the red-winged blackbird is the most common inhabitant, while in the scrubby stands of spruce and fir near the timberline, the white-throated sparrow reigns supreme. In open fields and meadows, grackles outnumber all other birds, and in backyards, around villages, and throughout suburban communities, the robin is number one. But in the vast expanses of hardwood forests that cover the majority of the Adirondacks, the most abundant bird is the red-eyed vireo.

Like the redstart and black-throated green warbler, two other abundant yet seldom seen birds, the red-eyed vireo spends much of its time among the dense layer of leaves in the canopy of these deciduous woodlands. Since it is no larger than a chickadee, and nearly the same green color of the leaves when seen from below, spotting one when it is perched on an upper limb of a mature hardwood tree is a challenging task. It is only when it flutters about, snatching small insects with its pointed bill, that you are likely to glimpse this prolific bird.

While nearly invisible from the ground, the red-eyed vireo reveals its presence with its constant singing. Its whistling sound is composed of a melodious series of notes that sound like

84

"cherry-o-wit cheree, sissy-o-wit, tee-ooh." While similar to a robin's call, the vireo's voice is higher in pitch, and its song lacks some of the robin's richness.

From mid-May until early July, the vireo's cheery song can be heard throughout the day. An ornithologist wishing to estimate the number of red-eyed vireos in an area need only stroll about and count the number of singing birds, especially during the early morning. In June, the song of red-eyed vireos is more common than that of any other species of bird, yet trying to pinpoint where it comes from is no easy task.

One of the reasons why this bird is so common in the hardwood forest is that each pair of nesting adults occupies such a small territory. All birds establish some type of territory which limits their numbers in a given area. Since the vireo lays claim to an exceptionally small plot of land, more pairs are able to take up residence in a set space compared to that of other bird species. (It has been extremely difficult for scientists to say for certain what the territorial requirements of the red-eyed vireo are. Few studies have been made of its nesting habits and behavior.)

While it spends much of its time feeding and singing in the forest canopy, the red-eyed vireo descends to lower tree limbs around the first week in June in order to build its nest. A forked branch of a sapling, or a small tree five to fifteen feet above the ground, are the preferred sites for its distinctively shaped nursery. Much like an oriole, the red-eyed vireo weaves a basket-shaped nest and works on it from the top down, rather than from the bottom up.

When in the vicinity of the nest, vireos keep quiet to avoid drawing attention to themselves. The veil of leaves that usually surrounds it causes most nests to go unnoticed during the breeding period. It's not until the autumn, after the branches lose their foliage, that they become visible.

Over the next several weeks, an observant person may notice a gradual decrease in the forest's bug population. Much of the credit for this goes to the insect-eating birds that come here to raise their families. At the top of this list is the red-eyed vireo, whose song is as much a part of the Adirondack forests as the squawking of the blue jay and the chattering of the red squirrel. Once familiar with its song, you will undoubtedly agree with most naturalists that this seldom seen creature is the region's number one avian inhabitant.

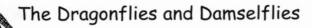

The Dragonflies and Damselflies

During the late spring, most insects become active, although few are as troublesome to humans as blackflies and mosquitoes. At this time of year, tiny caterpillars abound on the surface of tender, new leaves, or on the emerging foliage of ground plants. Similarly, immature crickets are eating and growing in mostly hidden nooks and crannies, although they won't announce themselves with their chirping song until much later in the season.

Among the most noticeable insects after Memorial Day are dragonflies and damselflies. Because of their large size and tendency to hover and fly about in areas frequented by people, they are likely to attract attention.

Both dragonflies and damselflies spend the winter as aquatic nymphs embedded in the muddy ooze covering the bottom of lakeshores, ponds, and marshes. After the ice thaws in April, these inch-long, wingless bugs resume an active existence. Initially, most of their time is spent searching for the tiny invertebrates upon which they prey. As they grow, they, in turn, become the target of other aquatic predators, especially fish.

Although similar in shape, damselfly nymphs are distinguished from dragonflies by their three paddle-like appendages on the end of their abdomen. Through these flattened structures they absorb oxygen from the water. Because they are twisted, they also help in underwater maneuvers.

Dragonfly nymphs are bigger than damselflies and absorb oxygen through tiny tubes which open into their abdomen. As water is pulled in, dissolved oxygen is filtered out. Occasionally the water is expelled from these tubes with enough force to propel the dragonflies several inches forward, helping them escape such prey as turtles, mallards, or sunfish.

Beginning in late May or early June, many of these nymphs metamorphose into their more familiar adult form. At this time, the nymphs climb out of the water. Some ascend plant stalks, others climb up objects jutting above the surface, and still others simply walk out to a dry spot along the shore. Their nymph skin splits open and out emerges the adult. Several hours later, their two sets of transparent wings are extended and ready for flight.

The way in which these insects position their wings when at rest is the main means of distinguishing between them. Dragonflies hold their wings outstretched, while damselflies fold them behind their back. Dragonflies also tend to have more robust bodies compared to the more delicate damselflies. Some people refer to the latter as darning-needles because of their long, slender abdomens.

Both species dangle their legs below their body when in flight, using them to capture airborne bugs. Blackflies, mosquitoes, house and deer flies, and assorted other small flying insects are routinely snagged and eaten by dragonflies and damselflies. (One researcher reported that a dragonfly caught forty bugs in a span of two hours.)

Each species possesses its own method of grabbing its prey. One is known to sit in the forest shadows until a bug flitters into a spot of light, at which point it darts out after it. Several other types can be observed cruising back and forth across a particular area patrolling for passing bugs.

While some people believe that these insects can inflict a painful sting, this is not the case. Neither dragonflies nor damselflies have the ability to sting, nor do they bite humans. But because of their size, they can hurt if you should collide with them when traveling at a fairly high speed. Standing in a fast-moving motorboat is the most likely occasion for experiencing such an impact.

Throughout June many types of dragonflies and damselflies begin to appear. Although they are not the most attractive insects, they are some of the most beneficial in terms of controlling the population of pesky flying bugs. Despite their appearance, they are harmless to humans and should never be killed simply because of their looks.

The Birth of Deer Fawns

In the Adirondacks, the peak birth season occurs around the second week of June. It is now that female ducks can be seen on a marsh, or along the edge of a pond, their young keeping a tight formation close behind them. Similarly, now is when you may spot a grouse hen crossing a road with her recently hatched chicks. Loon eggs also hatch around this time, as do countless mosquitoes. And as clusters of Indian paint brush and butter-cups tint unmowed lawns and the side of roadways orange-yellow, deer are giving birth to this year's fawns.

The peak of the mating season in the Adirondacks, as any big game hunter knows, occurs during mid-November. While some animals mate early and others late, the vast majority of does are bred during this time. Since their gestation period is one week shy of seven months, most does in the Adirondacks bear their young in mid-June.

Like other hoofed animals, the whitetail does not make a birth nest or den. As her time draws near, the doe seeks out a place of dense cover. Brushy thickets along the edge of meadows, patches of tall weeds in the tangled maze of alders, or a thick cluster of bracken ferns are favorite birthing spots.

In most areas across New York State does give birth to twins. In some western regions where the soil is rich and the plants are exceptionally nutri-tious, some does even have triplets. In the Adirondacks, however, the soil is relatively poor and the vegetation may lack some of the nutrients needed by the whitetail to maintain excellent health. The limited supply of browse, especially in winter, can compound this problem. As a result, some deer in these mature woodlands produce only a single fawn each year.

At birth a fawn is not much larger than a house cat and is unable to stand on its feet until it is about twelve hours old. It is a good week before the fawn is strong enough to travel with its mother. During this time, and sometimes even longer, a fawn spends nearly all of its time lying on the ground, tucked away under a clump of shrubs or in a pile of weeds. Its heavily spotted coat matches the pattern of bright light and shade cast on the ground by the leaves overhead, making it difficult for preda-tors to spot it.

For its first one or two weeks of life the fawn is also virtually scentless. Many forest carnivores, such as the coyote and black bear, which rely on their prey's scent to help locate a meal, find it difficult to sniff out a fawn. Because of this, the doe does not spend much time with her babies. Every three to four hours she returns to nurse them; but after they have received their fill of milk, she leaves so that her scent will not give away their location. But usually she remains close by and may attempt to distract animal intruders if they should stumble too near to her young.

Because of her fear of humans, however, a doe will not intervene if a person comes across her fawn. Occasionally, a good-hearted individual, noting that the mother doe is not around, will pick up the fawn to care for it or take it to a DEC official. Such acts, although well-intentioned, are most detrimental to the deer. The chances of the fawn surviving after being reared by a human and then released back into the wilds are much lower than those of deer raised by does. Unless there is a dead doe next to the fawn, most likely the mother is in the woods watching your every move as you approach her baby, waiting for you to leave so that she can return to it in safety.

There is something very special about seeing a white-tailed deer in the wilds. These graceful creatures seem to possess a magical quality that holds the attention of both avid nature lovers and those who have little interest in the natural world. In a few weeks, some lucky individuals will glimpse a doe leading her two-week-old fawn across the road, through the brush near a camping spot, or down to the lake edge for a drink of water and its first nibble on a tender aquatic plant. Until then, any fawn should only be admired from a distance and never touched.

June's Yellow Dust

In the second week of June, Adirondack residents and visitors alike may notice a yellow dust powder coating most outdoor objects. This film is especially noticeable on the windshields of cars, the surfaces of puddles, the tops of picnic tables, and on the water in quiet bays and sheltered shore-lines. Places adjacent to, or downwind from, a stand of evergreen trees are where this subtle film appears most pronounced, although it can be seen almost everywhere for about a week's time as the last threat of frost passes.

The source of this amber film is the conifer trees, particularly the pines, which spew billions of tiny pollen grains into the air as summer begins.

Like deciduous trees and wildflowers, the female evergreen tree requires pollen in order to form fertilized seed.

Unlike clover, honeysuckle, or apple trees, the softwoods do not rely on insects to carry their grainy, male cells from one plant to another. Instead, the conifers, like many hardwoods and some weeds, cast their pollen to the air and let the wind carry it to its intended destination. Since wind pollination is far less efficient than insect pollination, plants that rely on it produce vast amounts of pollen to ensure its target is reached. As a result, much of their energy and nutrients goes into manufacturing great quantities of pollen cells, rather than producing colorful blossoms used to attract bugs.

The sacs in which pollen is formed develop at the very end of twigs beginning in mid- to late May. These structures, properly known as male cones, are different from the swelling buds also located at the tip of the boughs that will soon add a new layer of needle-like foliage to the tree. As the leaf buds begin to open, the pollen sacs mature and release their colorful cells to the air.

The distance pollen travels depends upon the strength of the wind. On a breezy day these airborne particles can travel for miles, especially over open water or across fields or meadows. Trees high on a mountain spread their genetic information across nearby valleys, just as those on the edge of a lake end up fertilizing other trees all along the shore.

Although this yellowish dust initially floats on water, after a few days it will sink. Simply touching the water's surface with a stick, canoe paddle, or even your finger usually creates enough of a disturbance to send it to the bottom. In most bodies of water in the Adirondacks, pollen breaks down into its component parts. In bogs, however, decay is prevented by the chemical nature of the water. As a result, when the pollen sinks, it forms a microscopic layer which is preserved indefinitely. Each year a new layer, along with other material which falls into the water, is added to the bottom and forms a record of what pollen-producing trees were in the general area. Scientists that are interested in the forest composition of the Adirondacks hundreds and even thousands of years ago can obtain a record of the relative abundance of trees by analyzing the pollen from that era. Sifting through the muck brought up from the bottom of a bog to identify and count individual pollen grains may sound like an impossible task. Researchers, however, have been quite successful at this and have gained considerable insight into the nature of the Adirondack environment over the past several millennia.

Shortly after the pollen is released, tiny male cones drop from the twigs and accumulate on the ground, looking like scattered rice crispies. After pollination and fertilization occur, the seeds in the female cones begin their two-year process of development. (The cones that are commonly seen on trees are the female cones.)

The great number of pine and other evergreens in the Adirondacks add a dark green tint to the wooded landscape, along with a touch of grandeur. At this time of the year these trees also produce the amber coat cloaking exposed objects in this northern world.

The Precocious Porcupine

At birth all mammals and birds need parental care, yet the amount of attention that each requires varies greatly. Baby black bears are perhaps the most helpless, spending three to four months in a den with the sow before they are ready to confront the wilds of nature. Even then these cubs remain dependant upon their mother for both food and protection throughout summer and autumn. In contrast, some birds, such as grouse chicks or mallard ducklings, are able to feed themselves from the time they are hatched. Yet these infants rely heavily on their mother for more than a month to lead them to places where food is to be obtained and to teach them how to survive in a world full of predators. Perhaps the most precocious of all wildlife infants is the porcupine, which is able to fend for itself a week or two after birth.

Porcupines give birth in a den that can be found in any number of protected places. Large cracks and crevices between boulders or hollow logs are favored denning sites. Abandoned fox or coyote dens, holes in the ground, and abandoned buildings are other likely birth sites for this large, slow-moving rodent.

Most porcupines are born in the Adirondacks between mid-May to mid-June, while some births occur as early as late April and as late as mid-July. At birth, the baby (porcupines have only one per year) weighs around a pound, is about a foot long, and covered with moist hair. In the hours after birth, however, its hair dries and by the end of its first day of life it becomes very much like that of the adult.

Porcupines are well-known for their stiff, sharp, barbed quills. These quills are actually hollow hairs and cover only their lower backs, sides, and the upper surface of their tail. They are loosely attached to the skin and easily removed when embedded in another surface. Contrary to popular belief, porcupines are unable to shoot their quills. An attacking or inquisitive animal must make contact with the porcupine for the quills to become lodged in it.

When a porcupine senses danger, it tries to avoid confrontation by climbing up the nearest tree. If unable to do so, this near-sighted mammal turns its back to the intruder to expose its most effective weapons. By tensing the muscles in its skin, a porcupine can raise the angle of its quills. When in the presence of its mother, however, the skin muscles relax and the quills lower, preventing both parent and baby from becoming stuck or injured.

Because its quills protect it from most forest predators, shortly after its birth a baby porcupine is able to wander away from its den without the need of parental supervision. By its tenth day it adds to its independence by beginning to feed on tasty springtime plants. The bond between mother and young is not totally broken, though, for the porcupine continues to return to its home to supplement its leafy diet with some of its mother's protein-rich milk. It can nurse up to three months after birth; however, its nursing needs are dramatically reduced during the second and third month.

Young porcupines also tend to return to their den during the day to rest or avoid bad weather. Occasionally a young porcupine may stumble upon a shelter of its own and rest there for increasing periods of time rather than return to its mother's den.

While there are few dangers that face these infants, life for them is not totally carefree. Fishers, which are large and powerful members of the weasel family, pose a threat, as do coyotes, which can catch them unaware around the face or throat w h e r e there is only insulating hair. Disease and automobiles also take their toll.

Beginning in June, it is not unusual to see a young porcupine lumbering along the side of some back road, or inching its way up a tree along the side of a trail. The sight of such a small animal by itself might lead you to conclude that it must either be orphaned, or hopelessly separated from its mother. While such reasoning may be correct for the young of most other animals, it does not apply to this common Adirondack mammal.

The Mosquitoes Are Here

An abundance of rain during the late spring stimulates many forms of life. Moist weather provides mushrooms, molds, mildew, and other types of fungi with ideal growing conditions. Worms also respond well to a damp earth, as do many other soil invertebrates.

One of the most noticeable impacts of a spell of rainy weather in May or June is a rapid blossoming of the mosquito population. Like many insects, this ubiquitous bug has an aquatic stage in its life cycle. Puddles that exist for several weeks at a time in depressions on the forest floor are the ideal places for it to develop.

When the female is ready to lay her eggs, which can number in the hundreds, she searches for a stagnant pool of water. There the eggs are deposited on the water's surface to hatch. The amount of time it takes to hatch varies greatly, depending on the mosquito species and temperature.

The aquatic larvae which emerges from the egg appears like a miniature inch worm and makes a bending, wiggling motion through the water. During this stage of its life, the mosquito feeds on the rich supply of microorganisms existing in puddle water. On average, it takes about two weeks before they pupate and emerge as the familiar buzzing adults.

Prolonged dry spells tend to eliminate many of the temporary puddles preferred for the aquatic stages of life. During such times of drought, females are often forced to lay their eggs in far less favorable places, such as along the shores of lakes and ponds. In these settings waves and other forms of turbulence can destroy the fragile eggs and larvae, and expose them to a wide array of insect-eaters. In some situations a female may not be able to locate any body of water, thereby preventing her from reproducing.

Like blackflies, only female mosquitoes that have mated bite humans, other mammals, and birds. Pregnant mosquitoes require the nutrients in warm blood to foster the development of their eggs before they are laid.

Suitable hosts are located by means of tiny, yet effective heat sensors located near the tips of the females' feet. Because all warm-blooded creatures have a body temperature near 100 degrees, they stand out against the cooler surroundings by the heat which they radiate. This is especially true in the Adirondacks' cooler climate where such thermal differences are quite great. In open sunny places during the heat of the day, you may notice that few, if any, mosquitoes will bother you. This is because of their inability to discern you from inanimate objects that are baking in the sun. In the shade of the forest, however, the situation is far different. In such places a person's temperature contrasts well with the cooler background and begins to become most noticeable to a female in need of a meal of blood. At night mosquitoes are also far better able to locate a warm body.

To protect themselves from being harassed by these noxious insects, some nocturnal animals reduce the amount of heat which their body dissipates. Bears and raccoons, for example, still retain a rather thick coat of fur in summer and their developing layer of insulating fat keeps them from radiating too much heat. This helps to conceal them from the mosquitoes' heat detectors.

Some people may find it difficult to enjoy the beauty of the Adirondacks in the early summer because of the swelling number of mosquitoes. But there are ways to deal with this insect other than remaining indoors. Insect repellants are fairly effective when you are out hiking or canoeing close to shore. I suggest, however, that you simply lounge around in the sun where it is difficult for them to detect you. Frequent swims in the lake will help to reduce your surface temperature, also making you less noticeable.

When Bears Become Ornery

Few wildlife encounters create as much panic and terror as the sight of a bear out in the woods, or the sound of one nosing around your tent or lean-to after dark.

Because of its large size, powerful build, and the inaccurate publicity which it has received over the centuries, many people incorrectly believe that a chance meeting with one of these bruins in the wilds means that the person will end up as the bear's dinner. But anyone with knowledge of the black bear knows that this denizen of the deep woods and berry patches is not a human predator. In fact, wildlife biologists believe that the black bear has a far greater fear of people than we have of it.

Its fierce reputation and willingness to attack and kill large animals does have some validity, however. From mid-May until early July, this forest giant's docile disposition occasionally turns ugly. After it awakens from its prolonged winter sleep, the black bear immediately goes in search of food. Carrion tends to be the main item in its diet during April, as few other food sources are available to it. Although a bear ranges over a wide area, especially in the Adirondacks, its keen sense of smell enables it to home in on the thawing remains of any winter-killed creatures. It is the odor of food in the first stages of decay that occasionally draws bears into the outskirts of villages, especially on those days when bags of garbage await pickup by trash collectors.

By mid-May, all of the carcasses of dead animals either have been picked clean, or are no longer edible. As a result, bears are forced to rely on insects, worms, grubs, and other assorted bugs, along with the shoots of certain plants, as their main food sources. Although nutritious, such small items hardly satisfy the bear's tremendous appetite, forcing this part-time scavenger to occasionally turn into a predator.

During early June, most white-tailed deer in the region give birth to their fawns. While the fawns are nearly odorless during their first week or two of life, black bears have been known to follow the scent trail of the doe in order to find a helpless newborn. In one study of Adirondack deer it was noted that bears killed as many fawns as did coyotes.

In areas containing moose, the black bear is also known to repeatedly charge a cow moose with a newborn calf. While the mother attempts to remain close to her young when repelling the bear's violent attacks, she may inadvertently drift from the calf. When this happens, the bear immediately attacks the infant and makes a swift kill. Although an irate, 800-pound female moose can be a formidable force, the black bear, when hungry, is often willing to challenge this massive mammal.

Until berry season arrives, black bears are also known to attack and kill fairly large species of domestic livestock. Young horses, calves, lambs, and even full-grown sheep can be slaughtered and their remains dragged off into the woods by marauding black bears.

For most of June, the black bear's aggressiveness also extends towards other bears, since this month is its breeding season. As the summer solstice approaches, the male becomes increasingly ornery towards other males it may encounter in its search for food or a mate. Since its home range, which covers 40 to 120 square miles, may overlap with the ranges of other bears, chance meetings do occur.

Female bears, unlike all other Adirondack mammals, breed only once every other year. Sows caring for cubs that were born the previous winter will not mate until the following June. Should a male try to approach a female with cubs during this time of year, he will quickly be confronted with the fury of an incensed mother who knows that the male will make a meal of her cubs if given a chance.

It is a rare treat to see a bear in the wilds of the Adirondacks because of its wary nature around people. Although feared by every member of the wildlife community, humans have little need to worry about this black-furred goliath. Remember, however, a sow with cubs trailing behind her should always be given the right-of-way.

Spawning Sunfish

While gliding in a canoe near the shore of a quiet lake or pond, or while strolling along a trail that follows the edge of a bay or cove, various submerged items can frequently be spotted through the clear, shallow water. Rocks covered with a thin layer of brown silt, water-logged sticks with strands of algae dangling off them, and opened shells of fresh water mussels randomly scattered about, are all common sights in such settings.

Additionally, during the latter half of June in the Adirondacks, small circular patterns in the muddy debris can be noticed. These plate-sized depressions are the nests of several species of sunfish that spawn as the water warms.

In places where aquatic plants such as pickerelweed and pond lilies abound, it is the pumpkinseed that is the most common member of this family of thick scale fish. With its olive-colored back, green-streaked sides, yellow-orange belly, and bright red patch on its gill cover, the pumpkinseed is the Adirondacks' most colorful species of fish. Its oval shape and thin body combine to make this bony creature difficult to confuse with any other type of fish. Although there are numerous species of sunfish in the Adirondacks, it is the pumpkinseed that is traditionally thought of whenever sunfish are mentioned.

In warm sections of lakes and ponds relatively free of plants, the rock bass tends to outnumber the other members of this fish family. Longer and more robust than the pumpkinseed, this dark green and bronze-colored fish looks like a miniature version of its close relative, the smallmouth bass. Since both types of bass prefer life in quiet, rocky waters which support only a limited amount of vegetation, they are commonly found in the same general area.

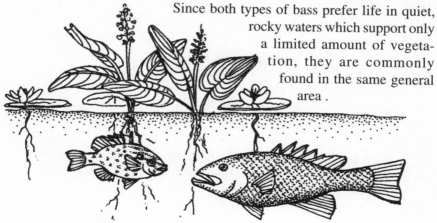

97

Despite the differences in habitat between the pumpkinseed and rock bass, both of these sunfish seek out shallow areas in which to spawn during mid-June. As is the case with the other members of this group, the male arrives first at the spawning sites. After laying claim to a particular section of the shallows, it brushes away the layer of organic debris with powerful strokes of its tail fin. The rapid sweeping movement is repeated until the gravely bottom of the lake bed is exposed. Ordinarily, the circular depression is no more than an inch or two deep, and has a radius equal in length to the male's body.

Once finished, the male will allow only adult females near the immediate nest site. Shortly after entering the nest, the female will deposit several thousand eggs, while the male swims along beside her to fertilize them. Typically, a female sunfish will spawn several times before exhausting her egg supply, and visit the nests of several different males before her spawning cycle is complete. As a result, the nest of a single male may contain tens of thousands of eggs from numerous females.

After the last of the eggs are laid, the male assumes the responsibility of guarding the rapidly developing embryos. The occasional movement of its fins, particularly the tail, creates enough of a current over the eggs to provide them with a suitable supply of fresh, oxygenated water.

After hatching, the fry, as they are called, remain in the circular depression for several days. Then these nearly transparent creatures move out over the rim to begin their life in the shallows, leaving the male free to return to a more productive feeding area. The wide array of tiny creatures that exist in the warmer sections of the Adirondacks' many lakes and ponds serve as their source of food. Few smaller forms of animal life are immune to their attack, and they feed almost continuously throughout July and August while the water temperature is most favorable to them. As the lakes cool, however, their pace of foraging slows. It has been reported by fish researchers that when the temperature of the water reaches 50° F, these colorful pond denizens become comparatively inactive.

After moving into deeper water, sunfish spend the winter as motionless as possible. Unlike some fish, these species do not form dense schools, remaining either in very loosely arranged groups, or by themselves. But as the water warms each spring, they become more active and resume harvesting the countless forms of invertebrate life that abound in the lakes. This usually aggravates serious anglers, and delights youngsters and others who simply enjoy catching fish.

JULY

Little Brown Bats Give Birth

Attics, darkened store rooms, and sheds are not only places for stashing relics from the past, they are also ideal roosting sites for colonies of little brown bats. During June and July, the females of this and a few other bat species congregate in such dimly lit, seldom disturbed spots to bear and raise their young. Known as maternal colonies, these clusters contain as many as a hundred or more bats, although a few dozen is the norm in the Adirondacks. The number of expectant mothers that occupies any one roost depends on the amount of available space, the number of other roosting spots nearby, and the availability of food.

The little brown bat, also known as the little brown *myotis*, is considered by many naturalists to be the most common bat in the Adirondacks. (There are eight other species of bats that occur in this region during the summer.) This small, delicate creature prefers to reside in places constructed by humans, while most other bats seek out cavities in hollow trees, large holes in the ground, or rock cubbies in which to roost. Several species perch upside down on a twig where the foliage forms dense clusters. There a bat may appear like a dead leaf or a clump of dried conifer needles.

The female little brown bat is more tolerant of hot places than nearly any other mammal, allowing it to survive in attics without adequate ventilation. One researcher discovered a colony of these bats in an attic with a temperature well over 120 degrees.

Mating season for all bats occurs any time after summer. Some bats mate during the autumn migration to their wintering roosts, while others breed only after their hibernating site is reached. Occasionally, little brown bats, like several other species, briefly awaken in winter to mate with a neighbor before returning to dormancy. Regardless of when breeding occurs, fertilization in the female does not take place until mid-spring.

As with most bat species, birth occurs during June or in the first week of July. Rather than hanging upside down, a female bat ready to bear her young will cling to her perch right side up. As the newborn emerges, it is caught and cradled in its mother's web-like tail. The little brown bat has only one young each year, compared to several different species that can have two or three young in a litter. For the first few days of life, the infant clings to its mother continuously and travels with her as she flies out to forage for food. But as it develops, it is left behind at the roosting site while the parent goes out for short intervals to acquire bugs.

Like all bats in this region, the little brown bat feeds mainly on insects. Mosquitoes, flies, beetles, and moths are the main items in its diet. Water surfaces are favored feeding spots for this and other types of bats, and it flutters about in meadows and forest clearings in search of food.

Because of its rapid digestion, a bat is capable of consuming large quantities of food in a short span of time. According to one bat researcher, after a bug is eaten, it is absorbed into the bat's system in slightly over a half hour.

By the time they are three to four weeks old, little brown bats are able to fly and quickly develop the skill of catching bugs in mid-air with their tail and wings. Soon after they are able to fend for themselves, the colony breaks up, usually in late July or very early August. Like the males, the females and young then adopt a solitary lifestyle, although several bats may still roost together.

Later in the summer, after abandoning their maternal roost, little brown bats spend the daytime wedged behind large chunks of loose bark on old trees, or in other protected places. After sunset they emerge from their shelter to feast on flying invertebrates.

Because of the females' delicate condition or because of their newborn offspring, a colony of bats in an attic, a cellar corner, or the recesses of a boathouse should not be disturbed at this time of year. If you happen to discover a bat cluster, leave them alone for the next several weeks and they will eventually disappear. If you do not want them there next year, then look to see where they are getting in and block off the opening after they leave. Remember, bats consume countless numbers of insects every night, and some folks who hate battling the bugs are of the opinion that there can never be enough bats around.

The Life of a Leech

Among the thousands of life forms that populate the Adirondacks in summer, only a few possess a naturally repulsive quality. Snakes and bats, for example, are creatures that most humans find rather grotesque, despite the very positive contribution each makes to the environment. Spiders, especially large, hairy ones, also upset many folks. One creature that few people wish to see close up is the leech. This aquatic *annelid*, closely related to the earthworm, possesses a more negative image than any other fresh water animal and can generate hysteria when it latches onto a swimmer's leg or foot.

Although commonly referred to as bloodsuckers, not all species of Adirondack leeches extract blood and body fluids from larger animals. Many leech types are actually predators and feed on the wide variety of tiny organisms that abound in quiet bodies of fresh water. Other species act as scavengers, consuming the tissue of animals that have died in the water or along the shore. In the Adirondacks there are several leech species that do act as parasites; however, only one of these is ever likely to attack a human.

Among the blood sucking leeches, most prefer a specific host, and a few restrict their choice to only one type of animal. For instance, one species will exclusively latch onto snails, while others are attracted to reptiles and amphibians.  These common leeches typically grab hold of the rear legs of frogs and turtles, as well as the lower back section of salamanders, where the host is unable to reach around to pull them off and eat them. Some leeches prefer to feed on fish, especially bullheads, because of their scaleless skin and their abundance in the muddy-bottomed waters where leeches reside.

Because they can be eaten by aquatic predators such as ducks, turtles, and fish, leeches tend to restrict their activity to areas that match their dark color. Those that stray into sandy bottom areas or places lined with light colored rocks are usually gobbled up in short measure. Places where the bottom is covered with a layer of muddy ooze are ideal, for they both conceal and provide shelter to burrow and hide in when the leech is resting.

Leeches are very slow to digest and assimilate nutrients. Some, after consuming a large meal, have been known to lie dormant in the bottom muck for an entire year before prowling again for another victim.

Parasitic leeches have a mouth equipped with three jaws designed to saw through the skin of their host. The teeth lining these jaws coat the wound with various chemicals. One substance dilates the blood vessels near the skin, causing a better flow of blood to that area. These secretions also prevent blood from clotting in the wound and help anesthetize that area so that the host is often unaware of the leech's presence.

In the Adirondacks, there is only one leech species drawn to humans. It is easily recognized by its olive-green back, marked with red and black spots, and its orange underside. It is common throughout the region's ponds, marshes, and lakes, as well as in the backwaters of rivers and streams.

If one of these leeches should latch onto a part of your body, there is no need to panic. (I know this is easier said than done.) Firmly pulling on this segmented worm is likely to break its hold on your skin with its rear sucker. This part has no mouth and is used only in maintaining its grip on its host. Once you have freed this back end, the front end may also let go. Do not attempt to yank it excessively, as its jaws may break off in the wound. If the leech refuses to relinquish its hold, then a little salt or a lit match may be necessary to change its mind. Once off, the wound may bleed because of the anticoagulants placed on it. Wash it thoroughly with soap and put an antiseptic covering over it.

July is the number one month for swimming in the Adirondacks. If you decide to take a dip in a place with some mud covering the bottom, do not be surprised to find leeches residing there. Remember, not all leeches parasitize humans. To be safe, simply go to a sandy beach, a place where rocks line the bottom, or swim from a raft.

The Pine Marten

The term Great North Woods is often used to describe the Adirondacks, and for good reason. Its forests are composed of a mixture of northern hardwoods and hardy species of conifers. Additionally, there are numerous creatures that reside in the region that are far more typical of the taiga areas to the north than the temperate settings to the south. Loons and mergansers, for example, populate the lakes, while the varying hare abounds in the forest underbrush. Blackflies, ravens, moose, and various other creatures also add to the Adirondacks' wilderness image.

One mammal associated with the cold-tolerant forest of evergreens and common in the backcountry settings of the Park is the pine marten. This little-known creature is only slightly larger than a gray squirrel, although it is noticeably different in appearance. Being a member of the weasel family, it is long and lanky, with short legs. It has a face somewhat like that of a fox, yet its snout is not as long and it is sometimes confused with a fisher, another member of the weasel family that also resides in the northern depths. The fisher, however, is roughly the size of a house cat. The ears of a marten are noticeably longer than a fisher's, and its fur is usually lighter in color.

Marten fur is exceedingly soft and thick enough to insulate it against the bitter cold of a sub-arctic climate. Trappers know this creature well, since its hide is used to make coats that are sold as sable. In some regions of North America the pine marten is referred to as the American sable.

Even though man is considered to be its prime natural enemy, the marten is less wary around humans than most other animals of the deep woods. Its unparalleled sense of curiosity occasionally causes it to leave an area of dense cover in order to get a better look at a camper or hiker. Like the black bear, it becomes especially bold when food is present.

The marten is an opportunistic feeder and will consume almost anything it comes across. Much of its time is spent hunting red squirrels, mice, voles, grouse, song birds, and other similar sized creatures that populate the forest floor and canopy. Because of its extraordinary climbing skill and its ability to maneuver among the branches of trees, the pine marten is as effective a predator in the trees as it is on the ground. Throughout the summer and early autumn, it will also feast on whatever fruits and berries are available. Neither carrion nor garbage is overlooked when the marten is on the prowl for a meal. At places frequented by humans, such as camping sites and lean-tos, the pine marten may stop by to check out what has been left behind, or to see if any edibles have been left unattended. Campers who leave their food out, especially at night, may awake in the morning to discover that their provisions have all disappeared. Black bears are well-known for their nocturnal raids on campsites; however, in the Adirondacks, particularly in the High Peaks, the pine marten is becoming more responsible for ransacked backpacks and torn supply sacks.

Suspending food from a rope that has been thrown over a limb well out from the trunk of a tree is the most common method of discouraging a bear from getting to your food. However, because of the marten's climbing skill, an extra measure must be taken in an attempt to foil its assault. Using a very thin nylon cord to suspend a food sack, rather than a rope, severely limits its ability to reach your provisions. However, the pine marten has become every bit as resourceful in raiding knapsacks as the red squirrel has in getting to bird feeders stocked with sunflower seeds. It is safe to say that no food pack is totally safe from attack if there is a hungry marten in the immediate area.

During July, the likelihood of seeing one of these sleek members of the weasel family increases, since this month is their breeding season. Over the next several weeks, the males will relentlessly travel over their territory in search of females. The female is believed to occupy a territory slightly less than one square mile in area, while the male's exceeds two miles. As a result, a single male may have the opportunity to breed with two, three, or even four different females.

The marten marks the boundaries of its territory with a potent musk produced in its abdominal glands. This scent also advertises its presence to other martens and makes it easier for a male to locate a female.

There are many forms of wildlife which occur in this wilderness area of New York. Because of their natural fear of humans, animals tend to remain out of sight when a person is in the immediate area. The pine marten is different, and is known to sit on an overhanging limb to get a better view of the hikers who walk below. If you plan on camping in a back country area, especially during July, take some precautions with your food, since this hardy little animal, which some campers have described as a "killer squirrel," likes to drop in uninvited to help itself to a free meal.

The Cicada's Summer Song

Not many animals respond favorably to the excessive heat that occurs in the Adirondacks during mid-July. On hot and humid days, birds concentrate their activities in the early morning or late afternoon and evening when temperatures are lower. Snakes find relief from the midday sun by slithering under rock in a cool, shady place. Fish, especially trout, become less active and travel to lower depths where temperatures are cooler. The cicada, however, is an insect that thrives as the mercury climbs. During the late morning and early afternoon, when the sun's heat is most intense, few sounds other than the cicada's loud, whining song can be heard.

Although its noise is a familiar part of the dog days of summer, the cicada itself is rarely seen. Since it produces its songs from a lofty perch in a tree, it is nearly impossible to spot when it sings, and because it is rarely on the ground, it is seldom stumbled upon.

The cicada is one of the Adirondacks' largest bugs, having a fairly large head and a robust body. It averages nearly two inches in length and has a set of transparent wings that cover its back. On the sides of the male's abdomen, a large membrane acts like the head of a drum, with muscles attached to it that cause it to vibrate rapidly. The sound is then amplified as it passes through a resonating air chamber making up most of the bug's rear body segment. The result is the familiar loud, whirring sound that lasts from fifteen to twenty seconds. At first, it is low in volume, then rapidly increases in intensity, remaining at a high level before again dropping off at the end.

A male uses its song to attract a female for the brief breeding period. After mating, the female then punctures the bark of a young twig and bores into the soft wood, cutting a deep slit in which she deposits her eggs. Each slit houses approximately two dozen eggs.

105

While this process protects the eggs, the gash weakens the young branch, often causing it to separate from the main limb during the next big wind storm. Several weeks after you hear a cicada calling from a tall maple, birch, or poplar tree, you may notice a dead twig or two in the tree's upper crown, evidence that cicadas eggs are lying in it. Although killing branches may seem harmful, some ecologists believe the cicada helps the tree through a process of natural pruning.

After the eggs hatch, the young cicadas, known as nymphs, drop to the ground and burrow into the soil, traveling down nearly two feet before finally attaching themselves onto the root of the tree.

Cicada nymphs have a mouth adapted for sucking juices from the roots of trees. Although the leaves produce the food for a plant, it is the roots that receive these nutrients for storage. Little is known about the impact made by cicada nymphs as they extract nutrients from the roots of trees. They probably remove such a small fraction that little harm is done to their host.

While underground, cicada nymphs occasionally encounter a mole tunneling through the soil. Because moles are fond of any type of invertebrate, cicada nymphs are quickly devoured. Those fortunate enough to avoid soil predators remain attached to the root for a prescribed number of years. Some species, such as the periodical cicada, may spend seventeen to twenty years underground before maturing into an adult. Other species have an eleven year nymph stage, while still others have stages lasting five to seven years. Other types may live underground for as little as two to three years. The cicada has one of the longest life spans of any insect.

In late spring or early summer, when it begins its journey to the surface, the cicada pushes its way upward using its front set of legs. With these appendages it pulls the soil down and then pushes it off to its sides. It then packs the soil into the wall of earth around it, forming a neat, circular tunnel. As a result, when cicadas reach the surface, unlike an ant colony, there is no pile of loose dirt.

Once they reach the surface, cicadas head to the nearest tree and climb up a short distance. There they hatch out of their nymph skin to emerge as winged adults. It takes the adults several days before they find the tree from which they will announce their presence. As the area swelters under the hot July sun, you may note a loud, whining sound coming from the upper branches of a nearby tree. This is the mating call of the cicada, a distinctive sound of an Adirondack summer.

 # The Appearance of Raccoon Cubs

From the time daisies cover open meadows and black-eyed susans line the side of roads, until the yellow plumes of goldenrod have faded, many wildlife parents are accompanied by their recent litter of young as they travel about. By following their mothers or fathers and imitating their actions, young creatures learn the ways of the wild. Coyote pups, beaver kits, deer fawns, robin chicks, and a host of other wild animal babies learn from their parents where food and shelter can be found and how to react in different situations. By mimicking their parents, the young develop the many skills needed to survive.

For raccoon cubs, the process of being introduced into the world around them and learning the many lessons of survival begins in July and continues throughout the summer. Although raccoons are born in the Adirondacks between the second week in April until the last week of May, these ring-tailed infants do not leave the safety of their den until much later in the season.

For the first month of life the cubs are helpless, and their eyes do not open until they are nearly three weeks old. During this period, raccoon babies, which number two to seven per litter, remain in their den under their mother's protective care. Seldom does she leave the den for very long, especially during spells of cold, wet spring weather which are all too common in this region during late April and much of May.

Because of their climbing skills, raccoons normally select a hollow trunk of a tree, well above the forest floor, to serve as their den. In some cases the attic of a vacant house or a loft in an abandoned barn can also be used. Such a high cavity ensures their safety from coyotes and domestic dogs, which are their principal enemies. Great horned owls, bobcats, black bears, and fishers also are known to prey on young raccoons.

By the time they are two months old, the cubs often poke their heads out of the den entrance and begin to practice their balance and climbing

skills by shimmying up the trunk a short distance or creeping out on a nearby limb. Around this time they also finally come to the ground, but only for short strolls, with their mother keeping a very close eye. At the first hint of danger the cubs instinctively head to the nearest tree and scurry up it. Should a raccoon become separated from its mother, it will emit a squealing sound, particularly if it is frightened, until its mother comes back for it. Both mother and cub will often call to one another by making a purring-twitter noise, especially in places of dense underbrush when they lose sight of each other.

Shortly after their second month, the cubs begin to accompany their mother on her nightly foraging trips. Since the water banks contain the greatest density of small animals, they are one of the first places visited by the raccoon family. Frogs, crayfish, minnows, tadpoles, and a wide variety of bugs are all commonly found along these banks. It takes a while before the cubs acquire the knack of capturing a moth with their front paws, or learn to grab junebugs, beetles, or crickets. However, the vast numbers of insects at this time of year make learning these skills quite easy.

Since the raccoon is an opportunistic feeder, it also frequents places where scraps of food are easily obtained. Bird feeders stocked with sun-flower seeds or suet and garbage bins are both places that raccoons quickly learn to visit. It is during this stage of their development that the cubs start to eat solid food. They will continue to nurse for the next month or two, but their dependence on their mother's milk begins to dwindle at this time.

By mid-August, the cubs are venturing out on their own for short noc-turnal trips, but they always return to their mother's den before daylight. Throughout autumn, juvenile raccoons travel to places visited during the summer, either by themselves, or in the company of a raccoon other than their mother. By exploring these familiar areas alone, and straying into other nearby settings with a neighbor, young raccoons learn where food is most plentiful and where danger often lurks.

When the cold weather finally settles in during late October or early November, young raccoons return to their mother's den where the winter is spent sleeping. After awakening next spring, the yearlings meander around their old haunts for several weeks before eventually striking out on their own. Now a year old, they either establish a home range of their own, or are simply driven from the area by their mother, who must make room for her new litter of cubs that will start this cycle all over again.

Visiting Gulls

Throughout the summer the Adirondack region attracts many visitors. The desire to explore the area's many lakes and waterways, dine at some of its fine eating establishments, and simply relax in the sun is not limited to people, however.

Gulls are also drawn to this section of the state from mid-spring until late autumn for the very same reasons. While countless numbers of birds travel to this mountain wilderness to breed, the gulls that are seen perched on boathouses, docks, and rocky islands, scattered along golf course fairways and athletic fields, and flying over villages, are here to eat, lounge around and enjoy the area, rather than to engage in any reproductive process.

Although commonly referred to as sea gulls, the birds that visit the Adirondacks belong to two species: the ring-billed gulls and the herring gulls. The ring-billed gull, which is more common around this region, is smaller in size than its close relative. It also bears a characteristic black marking around the middle of its bill, from which it gets its name, although this feature is difficult to see at a distance.

At times when large flocks gather at one location, there may seem to be more than just these two species, due to the number of different colored gulls that may be noticed. These birds are the sub-adults of both species. Like several types of other large birds, gulls do not reach maturity during their first year of life. Newborns are different in color from yearling birds, which in turn are different from the two-year olds. Herring gulls develop adult plumage near their third birthday, while ring-billed gulls reach sexual maturity

and support their own adult plumage a year earlier.

Before attaining adulthood, gulls travel far and wide, visiting different areas to explore. In summer, however, much of their time is spent sitting on large objects that overlook the water while basking in the sun. These juveniles are referred to by naturalists as "loafers," and the traditional places in which they hang out are called "clubs." There they have the opportunity to rest in the company of other gulls and bellow out their laughing-squawk as the need arises.

The adult gulls seen throughout the spring and early summer are mostly commuters that come from the massive breeding colonies on Lake Champlain, Lake Ontario, and the St. Lawrence River. Some naturalists believe that the ring-billed gulls restrict their breeding in northern New York to these colonies. As a result, these sites can contain tens of thousands of pairs of adult ring-bills.

While some herring gulls nest in small clusters scattered across the Adirondacks, most of these shore birds breed in massive colonies located in the major waterways that border northern New York. Since the areas around these island nurseries are unable to supply this many birds and their rapidly developing young with enough food, the parents are forced to forage well inland.

Because they are born for gliding, gulls usually travel long distances by riding thermal air currents. Like a soaring hawk, these off-white and gray birds circle effortlessly in an area of updraft, especially those created along mountain ridges. After gaining an appropriate altitude, they then head off in their desired direction. Some gulls are known to travel more than sixty miles to find food.

While dumps are favored feeding sites, these renowned scavengers are attracted to any place with a suitable quantity of garbage. Places containing fallen leftovers from picnics and camping trips are routinely visited by these birds, but more often they feed on small fish that wash up along the shore, along with beetles, worms, grasshoppers, and crickets.

Beginning in mid-summer, young gulls learn to fly and start to follow their parents to their feeding sites. Around this time the colony gradually dissolves, since the parent gulls now spend all of their time at their feeding sites, rather than traveling back and forth to a nesting ground. As a result, young brown and tan gulls begin to appear at gull clubs, and can be seen at parks, campsites, landfills, and beaches, where they start to fatten up for the colder season that is soon to come.

The Peak of the Berry Season - Blueberries

Summer in the Adirondacks is a time of many varied outdoor activities. None, however, is as rewarding to the palate and as satisfying to the stomach as berrying. Throughout the summer, there always seems to be one type of fruit or another that is just ripening. In late June and early July tiny, yet tasty strawberries come into season in open fields and uncut lawns. Toward the end of summer, wild black cherries develop, and although they are somewhat bitter, they can make a rather tasty jelly and an excellent flavored wine. Over the next several weeks the berry season reaches its peak as raspberries, blueberries, and blackberries ripen.

In open, sunny areas with dry, acidic soil, blueberries abound. Such conditions often occur under polelines or along stretches of abandoned railroads that cut through dense evergreen forests. Occasionally they grow on the side of some of the secondary roads in the North Country, and on rocky sections of lake shoreline where evergreen trees predominate. Additionally, blueberries are well known for recolonizing places in which fire has destroyed softwood forests, leaving the soil with little humus and plenty of acid. (The acids in which blueberries grow are produced by evergreen trees, not the polluting acids which, all too often, come with the rain.)

Their tolerance for poor soil conditions and severe climate allows blueberries to flourish atop the Adirondacks' highest peaks. When hiking above the timberline at this time of year, you may notice the presence of blue pea-size berries on the shrubs covering much of the ground. Nibbling on these tasty fruits during the end of July and the first half of August is an added enjoyment when taking in the view from a mountain summit.

Unlike their cultivated relatives, which can grow to be ten feet tall, blueberry bushes in the Adirondacks are dwarf shrubs that seldom attain a height of two to three feet. In places where conditions are favorable, they tend to grow outward rather than upward as dense, shrubby clumps.

111

Because they grow in the open, the fruits of these shrubs are exposed to the direct rays of the summer sun. As a result, they are often covered with a thin layer of white powder that helps protect them from the harsh ultraviolet rays which can be so damaging, especially to reproductive tissues.

Not all blueberries, however, have this powder on their fruits. A form of the late low blueberry, a common species in this region, produces berries that are black in color. Such fruits are often mistaken for huckleberries, which also bear black-colored berries. Although there are several botanical ways of distinguishing between these two closely related plants, I have found the most effective and rewarding to be an examination of the seeds. Blueberries produce many soft seeds within a single fruit that easily dissolve into the surrounding material when eaten. The berries of huckleberry, however, contain hard seeds known as nutlets, which give these fruits a seedier texture. They also tend to become trapped between your teeth after chewing on a handful of these berries. If you do not notice this you probably were feasting on black-colored blueberries rather than on huckleberries.

When hiking through the Adirondacks, it is important to note that not all blue-colored fruits are blueberries. Clintonia, also known as bluebead lily, is a flowering plant that grows abundantly throughout the evergreen woodlands. During mid- to late summer, this plant bears two to five purple berries that are the same size as blueberries. These fruits are clustered atop a foot-high stalk and should never be eaten.

While berrying may not be as exciting as water skiing, or as spiritually uplifting as mountain climbing, it can be just as rewarding, especially if you go with a good berry picker who doesn't mind your hand in his or her basket from time to time.

 ## Raspberries and Blackberries

While hiking along a backcountry trail, strolling past an undeveloped neighborhood lot, or simply working in a yard with a few shrubs, it is common at this time of the year to find ripening raspberries and blackberries. During years with a great deal of sun and rain earlier in the growing season, the arching branches of these thorny shrubs are usually laden with enough juicy, tasty fruits that few people are able to pass them by without stopping for a moment to collect several handfuls.

Like blueberries, raspberries and blackberries require a great amount of sunlight for growth. But, unlike huckleberries and their relatives, these brier-like shrubs grow best where the soil is rich and less concentrated with the tannic acid of the conifers. Abandoned pasturelands along the edges of farm fields, logged woodlands, and polelines that cut through upland sites are typical locations where these berries are plentiful.

Both raspberries and blackberries are quick to sprout and establish themselves in places opened up by human activity or natural forces. This is because the tiny seeds contained within each individual berry pass unharmed through the digestive system of most creatures. Therefore, after feasting on these berries, numerous birds and mammals end up depositing the inner seeds in their droppings, usually some distance away from the parent plant.

Those seeds that fall in places where the growing conditions are unfavorable, such as in the shade of heavily wooded areas, either fail to germinate or die shortly after sprouting. However, in places where there is plenty of direct sunlight, raspberry and blackberry plants begin to appear a year or two after the area has been opened up. Their first year of life results in the growth of one or more arching branches or canes that will flower the following year. It is from these flowers that the sought-after berries develop.

Many factors influence the number of berries that a plant will produce each year, and most have to do with the weather. If the growing season is too dry, wet, hot, or cold, or if there was an unusually late frost, the number of berries that develop is far less than normal. The abundance and activities of bees and other insects responsible for pollinating their flowers also have a great impact on the amount of fruit these plants bear.

After producing its berries, the stalk or cane will die during the coming autumn. Next year's fruits will form on the canes that sprout and develop this year. Both raspberry and blackberry plants have a root system that can live for many years, although their branches live for only a year and a half. In this way these plants respond most effectively from year to year to changing environmental conditions. If the amount of sun is plentiful and there is adequate water and soil nutrients, the roots will produce many canes. But if tree growth near one of these plants begins to cast increasingly greater amounts of shade over it, the plant will respond by decreasing the number of canes that sprout yearly.

In most places in the Adirondacks it doesn't take long for young trees, such as white birch and quaking aspens, to out-compete these shrubby plants for available sunlight. As a result, a thick patch of raspberries and blackberries can dwindle and disappear over the course of a decade or two. Many times a person will return to a favorite berrying spot after an absence of several years to discover that only a fraction of the former thicket remains.

Remember, too, that the berries can dwindle if a bear, a raccoon, a family of blue jays, or any other berry-loving creature beats you to the site. There are more wild creatures than most people imagine that enjoy dining on these tasty treats. Even animals not normally associated with eating plant matter, such as coyotes, foxes, and pine martens, can be found in a berry patch at this time of year attempting to pluck these fruits from their canes. While most creatures will flee from berry pickers, some may elect to stay and defend their feeding ground. In such situations, bears should always be given the right-of-way.

AUGUST

A Familiar Forest Inhabitant

Perhaps no creature is more watched as it moves about its territory gathering food and repelling intruding neighbors than the chipmunk. Around lean-tos and campsites, backyard decks, and woodpiles, the chipmunk is a very common animal that soon learns it has little to fear from humans. As a result, this ubiquitous rodent goes about its daily routine in full view of any camper, hiker, gardener, or homeowner that happens to be outdoors.

Although it belongs to the squirrel family, the chipmunk is not arboreal like the other members of the squirrel group. It spends nearly all of its time on the ground nosing about the layer of dead leaves and rotting sticks for the seeds of trees and shrubs.

When food is available on the forest floor, the chipmunk remains active all day gathering the fallen mast. In the Adirondacks, the winged, helicopter-like keys of the maples are the staple item in its diet. Beechnuts, wild black cherries, and several types of fungi are also important sources of food when they become available during the late summer and autumn. While raspberries and blackberries are eaten when they ripen, they are not collected for storage since they spoil easily. Likewise, although the chipmunk will dine on ground beetles and various other types of bugs and invertebrates, such animal matter is not placed in its underground cache either.

When the availability of dried seeds is limited, the chipmunk will greatly reduce its foraging activities until food can again be found. Should one crop of seeds fail entirely, this diurnal herbivore will become totally inactive until the next group of seeds mature.

When abundant, seeds are carried back to its burrow in its internal cheek pouches. Unlike other squirrels, the chipmunk possesses a pouch on both sides of its mouth capable of holding nearly a dozen triangular-shaped beechnuts. As a result, this packrat will stuff its mouth until its face bulges before returning to its burrow to unload the haul. During times of an exceptionally good crop of mast, the chipmunk may collect enough seeds over a period of several weeks to last for a full year. When food on the forest floor is limited the chipmunk will forage into its neighbor's territory as far as it can, while at the same time protecting its own territory more aggressively.

The only time the presence of another chipmunk is tolerated is during the very brief breeding season. In the Adirondacks, this occurs in early to mid-spring, or in early August. If food supplies are plentiful, a chipmunk may breed on both of these occasions.

Since the gestation period is one month, babies bred during July and August are born around Labor Day. The young develop in the confines of their mother's burrow for nearly six weeks before they venture into the world above. It is at that time, in late September and early October, that beechnuts ripen and drop to the ground, providing them with a rich source of nourishment.

While the appearance of a chipmunk during the summer is not a noteworthy event, observing the ebb and flow of their feeding activities, and noting their various types of behavior and social interactions, can be quite interesting. This is especially true around the first week of August when the urge to seek out a partner for the temporary mating encounter develops.

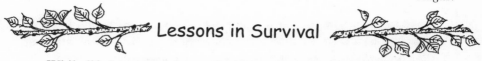

Lessons in Survival

While life is never truly carefree for any of nature's creatures, August in the Adirondacks is the time of the year when living conditions become most favorable. August weather tends to be cooler, less humid and more tolerable overall compared to that of July. There is also a reduction in the hordes of pesky insects that can make life so miserable during the early to middle part of this season. Additionally, as late summer approaches, the availability of ripened berries and mature seeds is at a peak, making for a period of feast, rather than famine.

Because of the temporary abundance of food, the population of many small creatures swells throughout the season. Mice and voles bear several litters each year, and the favorable food and weather conditions help promote their successful development. Likewise, the number of chipmunks, red squirrels, varying hares, shrews, jumping mice, and all species of birds is much higher during the summer than at any other time of the year.

For these young creatures, summer is the time to develop their survival skills. Learning where food is available and how to acquire it without being exposed to danger is what all creatures must master. For example, the concentration of edible plant matter during August makes it easier for an immature mouse to find enough food on its own to eat without facing starvation. The main challenge confronting such an inexperienced rodent is how to travel about the forest floor without announcing its presence to the owls, foxes, coyotes, and other creatures that also occupy the area.

The large number of snakes, wood frogs, salamanders, and numerous edible invertebrates focuses the attention of a predator away from a foraging juvenile mouse or vole. As a result, such young creatures have several months when the pressure of being hunted is substantially reduced, allowing them to develop their senses for detecting danger and the skills necessary for escaping natural enemies. Provided of course, that these immature creatures do not accidentally run into a more experienced adult.

Around this time, fox and coyote pups are also learning to find food for themselves. Early in the summer, the pups accompany one or both of their parents to learn how an adult goes about acquiring items to eat. After a successful kill, the parent usually shares the catch with its young. This introduces these future predators to the taste of meat, and teaches them that their hunger can be appeased by hunting.

The first solo attempts of a young fox or coyote to catch a meal are seldom successful. However, with repeated practice at locating, stalking, and attacking prey, their hunting instincts develop and their techniques for killing are refined. Additionally, the increased numbers of immature mice, voles, hares, and other inexperienced creatures helps improve the chances for a kill.

The presence of crickets, grasshoppers, berries, and other fruits throughout August provides the needed nutritional safety net for young predators to fall back on when they are unsuccessful in hunting, but after Labor Day, the availability of food begins to decline. Fortunately, by that time these pups, now nearly full grown, are no longer dependent on their parents for food. By the autumnal equinox fox pups usually depart their parents' territory to begin their search for an area that they can claim as their own. Although some coyote pups also leave their natal home, others remain in their parents' territory well into the winter.

The lessons of survival learned during the summer by both predator and prey are vital to their success. As the weather becomes colder and food more scarce, hunger can make a mouse less cautious in its search for something to eat. In such cases, it usually ends up as a larger predator's meal. Similarly, a young fox or coyote unable to deal with the dwindling food supply will also eventually die. The favorable conditions of August provide a reprieve from the difficulties of survival facing wildlife throughout the rest of the year.

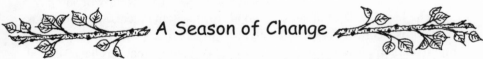

A Season of Change

As August progresses, an increasing number of signs, especially among the birds, indicates that autumn is approaching.

In the deep woods, a late summer silence has replaced the chorus of musical notes present only a few months ago. In open fields and along brushy forest edges, the chirps of crickets now outnumber bird calls. Although an occasional robin, white-throated sparrow, red-eyed vireo, or blue jay can still be heard, the cheerful melodious songs once sung by the vast majority of these avian inhabitants are now absent.

Since breeding time is over, birds no longer possess the urge to proclaim their hold over a particular plot of land, nor do they advertise their presence to a mate through vocalization. Territorial boundaries that were once vigorously defended by song, posturing, and occasional fights quickly dissolve by mid-summer. Rather than attempt to repel an intruding neighbor, birds now devote their time and energy to locating food. In some species, such as grackles, red-winged blackbirds, and robins, former rivals increasingly associate with one another in their search for items to eat, and eventually form small flocks. By mid-August, scores of birds can be seen flying overhead or foraging on the ground.

As the summer begins to draw to a close, some birds produce soft, simple notes. These quiet, inconspicuous calls are used by the members of a flock to maintain contact with one another, especially in areas in which dense, late season vegetation limits their vision.

Conversely, mid- to late summer is the time for crows to reassemble into large, temporary flocks that are anything but quiet. During their nesting period, crows tend to remain silent, unlike other breeding birds, to avoid drawing unnecessary attention to themselves. However, as soon as their nestlings develop into fledglings, they gather into flocks in which each bird tries to out-vocalize the others. During midsummer, crows spend the majority of their days in small family units scavenging for food. But by August, they increasingly congregate into these noisy flocks.

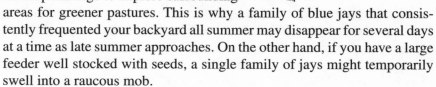

As summer wanes, changes in food availability also changes the behavior pattern of certain bird species. Rather than solely foraging for food around their now abandoned nesting site, some birds venture abroad. Young birds especially develop the urge to explore surrounding areas for greener pastures. This is why a family of blue jays that consistently frequented your backyard all summer may disappear for several days at a time as late summer approaches. On the other hand, if you have a large feeder well stocked with seeds, a single family of jays might temporarily swell into a raucous mob.

The dwindling food supply forces many birds to journey south. As cooler weather brings a welcome reduction in the number of flying insects, it also has an impact on the abundance of various insect eaters. Swallows, the first to leave for their wintering grounds in Central and South America,

119

begin their migration in early to mid-August, and will not return until the spring.

Hummingbirds, which feed heavily on flower nectar, begin their migration in late August or early September. At this time people with hummingbird feeders notice a moderate increase in the number of birds drinking from their colored, sugar-water containers. Such feeders serve as the last oasis for these tiny iridescent birds during the final few weeks of their stay in the Adirondacks now that many of their natural food sources are starting to fade away.

Although the weather will remain pleasant for the next month, birds are quick to respond to the many subtle changes occurring in nature, all of which point to the fact that fall is not too far away.

The Changing Robin

As goldenrod shares open fields and roadsides with light-purple asters, and as milkweed pods swell atop their tall stalks, subtle differences begin to occur in the behavior of the robin.

From the time it arrives from its wintering grounds in the early spring, until midsummer, the robin is drawn toward places with well-mowed grass, such as yards, golf courses, and parks. It is in such open areas that this common member of the thrush family searches for the seeds of grasses and weeds, as well as soil bugs and worms. It is especially active after the grass has been mowed. The lawn mower's rumble stirs many surface-dwelling invertebrates, making it easier for the robin to catch them. Lawn mower blades also act like thrashers, separating the seeds of the plant from the stalk as they chop them down and expel them. This results in a fresh supply of loose seeds, especially after untended lawns are mowed.

With the arrival of midsummer, however, the robin's attraction to well-maintained grounds starts to fade, replaced by its appetite for the wild berries in shrubs and on fruit-bearing trees now beginning to ripen. Choke cherries, blueberries, raspberries, wild black cherries, honeysuckle berries, and numerous other fruits are what the robin feasts on now, as it spends more of its time in brushy settings, or among the limbs of cherry trees than on the ground. Such foods fatten it up in preparation for its migration south and the leaner months soon to follow.

During spring and early summer, the robin's cheery song is the first sound to be heard as the sky along the eastern horizon brightens. And in the evening, its "cheerp-chererly-cheerp" tune, sung only by the male, is among the most common songs around Adirondack villages. But during mid-July, as the breeding season draws to a close, the robin, like other birds, seldom sings. (The exception is when it gives its "tuck-tuck-tuck" call to proclaim a situation of possible danger.) Instead, robins become sociable, in contrast to previous months, when the adults have little to do with other adults except for their mate. Although robins might simultaneously feed on the same athletic field or golf course, they are there not as a flock, but as individuals sharing a common feeding ground. As their second brood of fledglings begins to mature (in the Adirondacks robins raise two broods a year), they form small, loose flocks composed of a half dozen or more birds.

Beginning in August, robins from nearby areas assemble each night at a common site. Such a communal roost is often located in lowland areas, particularly in places where there is a dense covering of tall shrubs, such as in an alder thicket. From about a half hour before sunset until the sky is nearly black, a few small flocks sporadically congregate. Because they seldom sing, most nightly roosts go undetected by people in the area. At dawn the birds disperse, with the adults typically returning to the area that served as their nesting territory. The younger birds, especially the juveniles from the first brood, often go with other adults during the day in an attempt to explore the neighborhood and visit different surroundings.

As August progresses, the sight of a single robin perched on the lawn with its head held high and back gracefully arched becomes more rare. From now until early April, robins become more social and less musical, and more inclined to be in a tree or berry bush, than when they first appeared as the region's harbinger of spring.

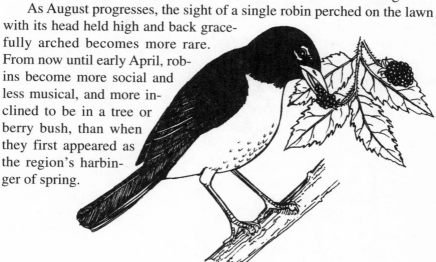

 # The Great Blue Heron

While the term "big bird" may conjure the character on "Sesame Street," it also brings to mind the great blue heron; a large, lanky denizen of open marshes and pond edges. In places where the water is shallow and the surface covered with spatterings of pond lilies, rushes, and pickerelweed, the sight of the Adirondack's biggest bird is not uncommon. While the recently reintroduced bald eagle has a larger wing span and is slightly heavier, the great blue heron still stands head and shoulders above all other birds.

Like the cranes, the heron is well suited for wading in shallow water. Its long, stilt-like legs enable it to walk from the shore into places where small fish, especially minnows, congregate. Its long toes adapt it well to slogging about in places where the bottom is covered with a dense layer of muck. Unlike waterfowl, the heron's feet are not webbed, since the suction that would result between a webbed foot and the muck, when walking in such places, would hinder its ability to move.

Another feature characterizing this bird is its long neck and long, narrow, pointed bill. Both of these attributes help it catch its food. Upon spotting some small creature in the water, it draws its neck back, then strikes, much like an attacking snake. Once in the clutches of its bill, the prey has no chance of escaping.

Although fish comprise the greatest portion of its diet, the great blue heron will dine on any small animal that makes the mistake of straying too near it. Frogs, salamanders, large aquatic bugs, leeches, and even mice are acceptable fare.

Upon returning from their wintering grounds in the

spring, each pair of great blue herons establishes a feeding territory. This usually is in the same marsh, section of river, or lake shore that the pair laid claim to the previous year.

Unlike most birds, the heron often makes its nest far from its feeding grounds, and like the gulls, is a colonial nester. All of the great blue herons in one general region establish their nests in a single, centrally located site.

The colony is always situated in a heavily wooded area not too far from one or more major bodies of water. Each tree within the colony, also known as a rookery or heronry, holds a half dozen or more nests. Because herons have difficulty maneuvering between closely spaced limbs, they build their large, circular nests among the outer branches near the tree tops.

Numerous colonies of great blue herons are scattered across the Adirondacks, with the largest ones just outside the Park, along the shores of Lake Champlain, the St. Lawrence River, and Lake Ontario. From each of these sites, the adult birds commute to their feeding territory, which can be fifteen to twenty miles away. Some travel even greater distances to reach a well-stocked marsh or pond.

Great blue heron nestlings are slow to develop compared to other birds. Almost a month passes before these gangly creatures begin to flap their wings, and another several weeks elapse before they are ready for their first flight. Initially, the young birds always return to their nest after a brief trip. It is not until they are nearly three months old that they abandon the colony, spending the remainder of the summer on their parents' feeding grounds or exploring other nearby aquatic settings.

Now no longer needing to return to the heronry to take care of their young, the adults are free to spend their time at a favorite marsh or pond edge. This allows them to acquire the fat deposits needed to fuel their migration south, and also explains why great blue herons are more frequently seen during the end of the summer than at the start of the season. Adding to their number are young birds now arriving at the feeding grounds for the first time.

Many natural signs reveal when summer will soon be drawing to a close. Around marshes and other shallow bodies of water, the increasing number of great blue herons is one of them.

The Chorus of Crickets

One sound more than any other typifies autumn's approach in the Adirondacks: the nearly ceaseless chirping call of crickets. In the weeks around Labor Day, these familiar musical sounds become as much a part of the background as the picturesque mountains and pristine lakes.

While crickets are more abundant earlier in the season, their cheerful choruses are seldom heard before August. This is because only adult crickets are capable of producing sound, and these dark colored insects generally do not mature until late summer, after meadows have turned yellow with plumes of goldenrod.

Like grasshoppers and katydids, crickets emerge from eggs in the spring and develop throughout the summer. Their eggs never hatch until the soil has thawed and warmed, which is usually during late April or in May.

Immature crickets are similar in shape to adults, except that they are smaller, unlike many other insects which experience a complete metamorphosis, and have larvae drastically different from the adult in appearance, internal structure, and often in their ecology.

During their nymph stage, crickets are concerned only with eating and avoiding being eaten by the many animals that dine on them. After developing into adults, however, the desire to breed quickly arises in these basically nocturnal creatures. As with many other animals, it is the male that attempts to attract a potential partner in order to carry out the mating process. This is done by rubbing the edge of one of its outside wings over the body of the other outside wing to produce a chirping sound. The hind legs play no role in their call, contrary to what most people believe. Also, it is only the male cricket that sings; the females remain silent.

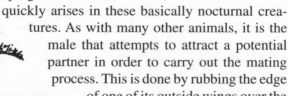

Although crickets are not capable of flight, they are equipped with two sets of wings, which become apparent when they sing. But other than to produce their mating call, a cricket's wings have virtually no function. Crickets jump, rather than fly, in order to avoid danger, and their large hind legs can propel them forward a fair distance when they are threatened.

Since the cricket's activity, like that of any bug, depends on the warmth of its surroundings, the number of chirps that this insect produces in a given period of time varies with the temperature. On cool evenings when frost is possible, their chirping is markedly slowed. On warm nights, however, they chirp rapidly, and when several males are clustered together, it is difficult to distinguish between individual chirps amidst the constant chorus.

Female crickets are able to detect the love songs of the male by special auditory organs which are located on the middle section of their front legs. These "ears" are tuned to the chirps of a particular species, allowing a female to single out a suitable male from the multitude of other types of crickets singing in the same area.

After mating, a female will deposit her many fertilized eggs in the surface of the soil. If left uneaten by the birds, shrews, and other animals foraging about, they will hatch into a new generation of crickets the following spring. In all species of crickets, the eggs must pass through a lengthy period of below freezing temperatures before the embryos inside can develop and hatch in the spring.

There are many types of crickets, resulting in the variety of chirping sounds. One species of cricket not found in the Adirondacks, however, is identified by its suit coat, tie, top hat, and umbrella. This type of cricket is frequently accompanied by a cute wooden puppet with a variable length nose. If you should ever happen to encounter such a duo, you will note that the voice of this cricket sounds more like the whispers of one's conscience than the pleasant noise that is so familiar at this time of year.

An Unwelcome Nocturnal Visitor

Few animals pose a greater threat to the peace and pleasantness of a neighborhood than a skunk. Unlike many Adirondack creatures, the skunk is not a denizen of the deep woods, preferring to reside in overgrown meadows, fields, or well-manicured lawns. As a result, many of the skunks in the Adirondacks live around its towns and hamlets.

For much of the summer, the skunk spends its nights foraging along the sides of roadways and under powerlines, where berry bushes abound. Although this dorsal-striped member of the weasel family has a definite fondness for dining on animal matter, it will eagerly consume the juicy fruits found on the low shrubs and thorny brambles of forest edges and woodland clearings.

As August progresses, the number of berries diminishes, causing the skunk to amble into areas with a greater assortment of food items. Among these are mowed lawns and cropped fields, where it can dig in the rich soil for bugs.

During summer's peak, the ground surface in open areas can become quite dry and its temperature can soar. Although some bugs still reside there, many go deeper into the soil, where moisture and temperature conditions are more favorable. Other invertebrates escape this adverse situation by entering a stage of their life cycle that causes them to temporarily seek out other settings.

During late August, as more frequent showers occur and cooler temperatures prevail, the uppermost layer of soil in fields and lawns becomes a more hospitable place for bugs, which in turn attract skunks as autumn approaches. With their sharp claws and stubby legs, skunks can easily tear away a small clump of sod in order to uncover the bugs beneath it.

Lawns free of skunk activity in the spring may now show signs of being a regular skunk stopover as skunks born in the spring begin to venture out on their own. These juveniles will explore a variety of different areas in their search for a territory they can claim for themselves.

Along with wrecking lawns, the skunk also makes a nuisance of itself when discouraging a neighborhood pet from getting too close. This slow-moving creature relies almost entirely on its chemical weapon to protect it while it is out of its den. Since many of its enemies have a keen sense of smell, a snoutful of this potent musk can be more traumatic to other animals than most people imagine.

When confronted by an intruder, a skunk first stomps the ground with its front paws and growls to show its displeasure. If the intruder does not retreat, the skunk quickly turns its back, lifts its tail, and discharges a thin stream of musk directly at its target. Skunks are extremely accurate with their discharge, even when faced with rapidly approaching attackers. Even baby skunks can shoot musk with a good deal of accuracy.

After traveling about ten feet, the musk disperses into a very fine mist that covers a much larger area. Even though the intruder receives the brunt of this musk on its fur, there is always a portion that lingers in the air well after the encounter, much to the annoyance of any passersby.

Skunks are also known for helping themselves to the contents of trash bags left alongside a curb. If there is edible matter in the garbage, a skunk will consider it fair game. Care should always be exercised when dealing with a skunk pawing through your garbage, or ripping small chunks out of your lawn. There is always the possibility that any wild animal is rabid, and in recent years the number of cases of this viral disease in skunks has increased dramatically. To be safe, stay a good distance from all forms of wildlife, especially ones that can launch an attack with an extremely potent, chemical weapon.

 ## The Peak of Yellow Jacket Activity

There are only a handful of insects that are annoying when you are engaged in outdoor activities in the Adirondacks. During the late spring it is swarms of black flies, while in summer, both deer flies and mosquitoes are the biggest culprits. In August and early September, yellow jackets become the primary disrupters of a peaceful outing. As the population of these amber and black stinging insects reaches its peak, they increasingly frequent backyard barbecues, picnics, or other functions where food is present.

Unlike bees, which live through the winter and begin life where they left off the previous autumn, very few yellow jackets survive the long winter. Only fertile females born in late summer, which have left the colony, mated with drones, and found a safe shelter, usually in a place of loose soil, can survive this time of bitter cold.

Upon emerging from their dormancy in the spring, these fertilized females begin the task of establishing new colonies. The first requirement is locating a suitable nesting site. Unlike other hornets, which suspend their papery nests from branches of trees or the eaves of a house, yellow jackets make their paper nurseries in shallow holes in the soil. While some excavate their own cavity, others set up housekeeping in unused mole tunnels, abandoned chipmunk burrows, or in the deserted subterranean chambers of mice or voles.

127

After digging or finding a suitable hole, the queen builds about a dozen hexagonal cells. These are manufactured out of a type of paper which hornets produce by mixing mouthfuls of partially rotted wood with their saliva. Once this honeycomb is completed, a single egg is laid in each of its cells. In a few days these eggs hatch into tiny, caterpillar-like larvae with a ravenous appetite. Unlike adult yellow jackets that feed mainly on flower nectar and other sweetened plant juices, larvae must be given foods rich in animal protein. During the spring, the queen tries to locate the remains of winter-killed mammals or birds, or a bag of open garbage. Otherwise she must hunt insects, spiders, or centipedes.

All the larvae that emerge from these cells are females, or workers. They immediately assume the many chores previously performed by the queen. Six weeks after establishing the colony, the queen usually has produced a sufficient number of workers so that she can settle down to the sole chore of laying eggs.

Yellow jacket colonies can expand greatly in size during early to mid-summer. A nest that originally was only an inch in diameter metamorphoses into one the size of a volleyball, containing hundreds of adult females. (Pity the poor soul that runs over one of these with a lawn mower.)

Because the larvae contained in these cells are rich in nutrients, they are the target of several forest predators. Skunks, raccoons, and bears all have been known to tear apart yellow jacket colonies at night, when hornets and wasps are inactive, in order to feast on their larvae. While they are often repeatedly stung in this process, these tough skinned creatures don't seem to mind, continuing to plunder yellow jacket nests whenever they stumble upon them.

By late August, the deposit of sperm in the queen begins to dwindle and she starts laying unfertilized eggs which develop into males or drones. At this time many of her fertilized eggs develop into fertile females, rather than workers. Entomologists are still unsure why this is so. Some believe that it is due to a change in their diet during this season, while others think a temperature difference triggers the formation of new queens.

Shortly after they emerge as adults, both the drones and future queens depart the colony. After mating, the males die and the now fertilized female attempts to find a place to spend the winter. Back in the colony, as cooler weather sets in, the workers, along with the old queen, begin to die. By the time the leaves are off the trees, most will be dead, leaving only the new queen to start another generation of yellow jackets for next year.

SEPTEMBER

The Mushroom Season

As blackberries begin to wane in brier patches along forest clearings, mushrooms become ready to harvest throughout the Adirondack woodlands and fields. Early September is the peak of the mushroom season, offering numerous types of fungi every bit as pleasing to the palate as the juiciest berries.

Unlike green plants, mushrooms do not thrive in warm, sunny weather, favoring cooler days around 60° F and dwindling amounts of daylight. Proper moisture is also critical to these plants. The rains of early autumn and days of heavy dew well into morning are ideal for the growth of these fungi.

As with edible plants, the part of the mushroom that is eaten is the section associated with reproduction. Known as the fruiting body, the sole function of this creamy-white structure is to bear the plant's many one-celled seeds, called spores. Most fungi produce tens to hundreds of billions of seeds, with some puff balls producing as many as several trillion.

Although some mushrooms grow to be fairly large, most of these primitive plants lie beneath the soil, or under the rotting stumps or decaying limbs on which the fruiting body has sprouted. The vast majority of these plants comprise an intricate network of thin, thread-like filaments that permeate the material in which the mushroom grows. Known as the *mycelium*, these fragile strands develop during the summer and can be seen when carefully sifting through soil. Dark soil mixed with decaying leaves and needles often reveals mycelium threads when examined closely.

129

A cluster of mushrooms in a small plot of ground most likely comes from a single, yet extensive *mycelium*, much like the multitude of flowers that form on a plant.

Because mushrooms are unable to carry out photosynthesis, they must rely on alternative sources of nourishment. Their fibrous bodies either act directly on dead matter or absorb the energy-rich products of decay suspended in water within the soil. A few mushroom species have a symbiotic relationship with the roots of certain trees, especially conifers. Such fungi readily absorb mineral-enriched water from the soil and pump it into the tree roots. In turn, the roots provide the mushrooms with food manufactured in the trees' needles and leaves. These types of mushrooms are always associated with specific trees. The poisonous Fly Agaric mushroom, for instance, is found under conifer and hardwoods as is the edible King Bolete, which most often occurs under the Norway spruce.

When harvesting mushrooms it is important to know which ones should be left alone. In the Adirondacks some are very toxic, while others taste very fine. Some connoisseurs claim that the King Bolete is superior in taste to any type of commercially grown fungi.

Because they are common and easy to identify, boletus mushrooms are perhaps the most sought of all the fungi. Not all bolete mushrooms, however, are good to eat. The Redmouth Bolete, which grows in hardwood and evergreen forests, is poisonous. This is why it is imperative to know proper mushroom identification before you go harvesting. However, once you are positive of a specimen's identity and are assured of its edibility, never hesitate to sample a wild mushroom. Because each person's taste varies, what one individual may report to be only fair in taste, another may find irresistible.

When hiking or strolling during this time of year, take note of the various types of mushrooms you see. With a little time, some careful examination, and consultation of a good guide, you will add greatly to your outdoor experience.

130

 **The Muskrat's Autumn Routine**

With the arrival of Labor Day, several seasonal changes transpire in the Adirondacks' many marshes. The bugs so evident only weeks before now are scattered and few. This causes the swallows that conspicuously sailed and glided over the water and its surroundings during the preceding months to retreat to more southern regions. Solitary ducks are also seldom seen this time of year, as waterfowl begin appearing in pairs or flocks. And beginning in early September, summer's lushness fades from the leafy plants standing above the water's surface. As these plants wither and die, small cone-shaped mounds of their discolored stalks and shriveled foliage begin to appear among the remaining patches of grasses and weeds. Usually spattered with a coat of mud from the bottom, these heaps of green and brown plant matter often rise several feet above the surface, the workings of the muskrat, the marshes' most prolific mammal.

As fall approaches, the muskrat prepares for the coming winter, with shelter its main concern. Although it spends much of its life in the water, the muskrat, like the beaver, requires a protective place above the water line in which to rest. Commonly referred to as a muskrat "house," it is located in one of two distinct settings.

In places where a relatively high bank exists close to the water's edge, the muskrat makes its home in a burrow along the shore. Although suited for a life in the water, this rodent is also well equipped with very sharp claws for digging. Upon selecting a suitable site, it begins constructing the entrance to its future living quarters by digging into the bank below the water line. Like a beaver lodge, the underwater entrance to a muskrat house provides protection against unwanted intrusions by other creatures. After tunneling several feet into the shore, the muskrat then angles upward until it is above water, then enlarges the burrow to create a cavity that it lines with pieces of soft vegetation.

Since the hilly terrain of the Adirondacks causes most bodies of water to be close to elevated sections of shore, many muskrats live in a chamber excavated in the side of a bank. Its preference for life in an earthen enclosure often prompts the muskrat to tunnel a dozen feet or more underwater to reach a suitable bank.

In flat landscapes, or within large marshes set away from dry land, the muskrat is forced to construct a house in a massive pile of mud, weeds, and

131

grasses, which it must then assemble. Such a residence is similar in shape and design to a beaver lodge, although it is not as large.

In addition to its primary shelter, most muskrats also build one or more smaller feeding shelters at this time of year. These are nearly identical in shape to their weed and grass homes, except that they are not as massive or as sturdy. These covered eating areas, too, can only be entered through an underwater tunnel.

These temporary shelters both conceal the muskrat from roving predators and protect it from the night's chill air. Despite its thick coat of fur (which has made the muskrat a popular target for trappers), this nocturnal creature is sensitive to freezing temperatures and blustery winds. As a result, as autumn progresses and the mercury drops, it stays sheltered, consuming the succulent stems, leaves, or tubers that it collected during its underwater forays.

After Labor Day, juvenile muskrats begin their search for a place to spend the winter. In the Adirondacks, muskrats average three litters per year. The first is born in mid-spring, the second in early summer, and the third sometime in August. While the young of the preceding litter are usually forced out of their parents' territory just before or shortly after the female gives birth again, they tend to remain in unoccupied sections of the marsh. Often such places are ideal for the summer, yet become totally uninhabitable when ice begins to form later in the season.

As autumn progresses and the breeding season comes to a close, territorial boundaries are not as vigorously defended as in spring and summer. This allows maturing muskrats the opportunity to explore the region without being viciously attacked by the normally possessive marsh-owner.

Once it has found an unoccupied section of marsh where it can survive the winter, the muskrat starts work on its home, and then on a feeding shelter, if necessary. Occasionally, a wandering individual will find a corner of a marsh that has been unoccupied by these scaly-tailed creatures for a year or more. In such cases, a mud and weed hut might suddenly rise among the dying stalks of cattails and reeds. This could be the muskrat's home or just a feeding shelter. Only an expert naturalist or a muskrat knows for sure.

The Autumn Migration

Coinciding with the exodus of summer residents and vacationers is the autumn migration of many of the Adirondacks' birds, which now depart the region for more favorable environs. The tree swallows are among the first to leave, congregating into flocks during late July, and then disappearing a few weeks afterwards. Most birds, however, wait until September before starting their southward journey. This allows them the opportunity to do nothing other than eat, now that they have completed the task of rearing their young. Because such a long trip requires a tremendous expenditure of energy, migratory birds tend to build up as much fat as possible prior to their departure. Robins, for instance, commonly feast on the wide assortment of wild berries throughout August and early September to acquire the nourishment needed for their trip. During the middle to end of summer, flocks of grackles and red-winged blackbirds descend into fields and pasturelands to dine on the grass and weed seeds available there.

Some birds, such as gulls, linger well into the autumn in accumulating a substantial fat deposit. Loons, ducks, and great blue herons also remain after most of the other birds have left. Some of the more hardy of these aquatic birds won't leave until ice starts forming on the edges of marshes and the shores of lakes.

As their principle sources of food dwindle down, birds are quick to take advantage of favorable migratory weather. Strong northerly winds are ideal for southward migration. A stiff breeze can greatly facilitate air travel, often adding five to ten miles per hour to the bird's flight speed. On calm, pleasant days, or when there is a warm breeze out of the south, many migratory birds remain in their preferred habitat, regaining the nourishment lost during a long period of travel. As a result, the retreat of birds to warmer settings occurs in spurts, much like the departure of area visitors on Labor Day weekend.

Although nearly all birds are diurnal, more migrate at night than during the day. Most of the songbirds, such as the warblers, vireos, thrushes, and sparrows are nighttime travelers. Others, like geese and ducks, prefer to fly during the day, yet will continue to fly southwards throughout the night if northerly gales are blowing. Night travel allows the birds the opportunity to feed during the entire day, which is often necessary for such small and active creatures.

Unlike geese, which fly high in the sky when they pass overhead, most common migrating songbirds only fly about a hundred feet above the tree tops. Because their eyes are not adapted for night vision, these sojourners often fly into tall, man-made obstacles once darkness settles. Tall radio towers, guide wires, and high voltage power lines are among their greatest hazards.

Only a few birds, like the swallows and chimney swift, do their traveling during the day. Because they rely almost exclusively on flying insects for food, they are able to feed and migrate simultaneously. The swooping and banking type of flight needed to catch bugs while on the wing, however, impedes their southward progress. As a result, their erratic style of flight covers only a dozen or so miles per day.

Nighttime migrants, on the other hand, cover a much greater distance, as their flight is much more direct. While songbirds can rapidly move through the air when disturbed by an intruder or pursued by a predator, they pace themselves on long distance excursions. It is estimated that common perching birds wing their way to their wintering grounds at a rate of twenty miles per hour. Thus a flock of robins, blackbirds, or starlings that departed the Central Adirondacks on a blustery evening can be in southern Connecticut, New Jersey, or Pennsylvania by sunrise the following morning.

The Social Chickadee

While the vast majority of birds that breed in the Adirondacks are migratory, some species remain throughout the year despite winter's harshness. Nuthatches, several varieties of woodpeckers, the evening grosbeak, and the purple finch remain year around, yet no permanent resident is as familiar and well-liked as the black-capped chickadee.

The fact that the chickadee is always seen in flocks reinforces the friendly image that humans have of it. Additionally, its soft voice gives this small, fluffy creature a warm and cheerful personality. The chickadee's social nature and vocal qualities also enhance its ability to survive in the northern forestlands.

Like nearly all birds, adult pairs of chickadees maintain breeding territories during much of the spring and summer. However, as soon as the nesting season ends, and the fledglings are able to fend for themselves, small flocks gradually form and remain together until the following spring.

While some birds form flocks numbering into the dozens, and sometimes even hundreds, a typical flock of chickadees contains only six to ten birds. Ordinarily, two to three pairs of adults that nested near to one another congregate during the latter part of the summer to form the nucleus of the winter flock. From late August to mid-September, they are joined by several of the year's young that have wandered into the area. (Immature chickadees will disperse at least two to three miles from the location where they were hatched.)

During these last weeks of summer, the flock establishes a winter feeding range that usually encompasses the former breeding territory of the adults in the flock. Boundaries are fixed and each band of birds will defend its domain against the intrusion of neighboring flocks. By remaining vigilant for trespassers, chickadees are able to quickly detect the presence of a predator that might also have entered the area. A flock of these gray, white, and black birds is far better able to detect danger than any single creature in the forests. This is particularly so in evergreen woodlands, where snow-covered boughs of spruce, fir, and pine severely limits an animal's visibility, enabling a predator to sneak up on its quarry.

Once one member of the flock spots a possible source of danger, it immediately alerts the others with a call of alarm. Because this greatly reduces the chances of a hawk or pine marten from launching a surprise attack on any one member of the flock, other species of birds often tag along with chickadees as they forage through areas of dense vegetation. Migrating warblers are especially well-known for seeking out a flock of chickadees in order to feed

135

with them in a stand of conifers.

Since they are frequently out of sight of one another, flock members rely on vocalizations to notify the others of their approximate location. This helps keep the flock intact and prevents individuals from straying too far from the group when feeding.

As the flock forms, a pecking order develops, with each flock containing a dominant male and female, along with various levels of subordinates. The older birds are typically at the top of this hierarchy, while the juveniles occupy its lower end. As is the case with wolf packs, the leaders eat first or whenever they feel like it when the flock happens upon a single source of food. This explains why one bird may be seen taking its time at a feeder while the others wait patiently in nearby branches. And why one bird may land at the feeder only to immediately give up its spot to another before taking a seed.

In exchange for being last in line for food, the young birds gain valuable knowledge from the flock's elders, learning where natural supplies of food exist, as well as where bird feeders are located.

While there is safety in numbers, chickadees are not impervious to attack. Periodically, one of their natural enemies (usually a hawk) is successful in raiding the flock and plucking one of these social creatures from its perch. By the early spring, a flock is often reduced to only four to six birds, which is the number that most areas will support when the breeding season comes around again the following year.

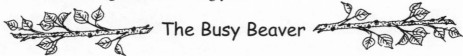

The Busy Beaver

Upon viewing a beaver pond, you can easily understand how this animal has acquired its reputation as a dedicated, hard-working animal. The many pointed stumps about the shore, along with a litter of three- to four-foot long sticks and limbs stripped clean of bark, serve as a testimony to its industriousness. A beaver will gnaw on a tree until it has not only toppled it, but has cut it into easily transported sections. The occasional canal that extends into a lowland alder thicket or muddy, brush-covered flood plain illustrates the beavers' willingness to dig wherever it may be to their benefit. The massive size of their cone-shaped lodge, composed of intertwined sticks packed with a layer of mud, demonstrates their talent for erecting a well-insulated, fortress-like chamber.

Unquestionably, their most impressive feat is their dam, which can impound millions of gallons of water to create a pond in which the beaver family lives. Such a barrier of sticks, leaves, weeds, rocks, and mud can extend for well over a hundred feet and stand up to three feet high, depending on the lay of the land.

Although it remains active all year, the beaver accomplishes the most in the autumn, until there is a hard surface of ice on its pond. During the rest of the year, it cuts few trees. As soon as new vegetation begins to sprout along the shore in early May, the beaver forgoes its diet of poplar, birch, willow, and alder bark in favor of more tender, leafy plants. The shoots of cattails, the stems of pond lilies, and the blades of various aquatic grasses are its food during the warmer months of the year.

While it retreats into its lodge during the daylight hours, the beaver makes no improvements or repairs to its house in summer. Likewise, its dam is often given little attention during this season. It is only in early September that it prepares for the coming winter. As the sap starts to flow from the wood, this sharp-toothed animal cuts down, chops up, and hauls back toward its lodge more and more trees. While some of the branches are used to reinforce its house, most are pushed into the muddy bottom just outside the underwater entrance, where they will serve as its winter food reserve. Recent research indicates that this activity is performed during the first half of the evening. The second half of the increasingly long night is spent digging canals into areas in which food is abundant, coating the lodge with mud, and working on the dam.

A pair of beavers moving into an unoccupied section of stream, usually in May, are able to erect a sizeable dam in one or two months. Once a framework of sticks anchored in the mud on the stream bottom is in place, Mother Nature begins to help with the dam construction. Freshly fallen leaves and twigs knocked into the water by autumn winds are carried by the current and become entangled in the lattice of branches already in place. Additional limbs are wedged in by the beavers night after night, and

weighted down with rocks placed on top of them. Silt and sediment become trapped in this barrier, further reinforcing it and waterproofing it. By mid-November, a fair-sized dam can be in place on a stream or brook that was free of such an obstruction on Labor Day. By Thanksgiving, most of the beavers' chores are completed. As the ice becomes thicker, the movements of this flat-tailed mammal diminish. Most of winter, spring, and summer is spent either resting, sleeping, swimming, or eating. There is no doubt that beavers are busy, hard-working creatures this time of year. Anyone on a highway crew will attest to their knack for continually plugging up culverts and damming streams near roadways during September and October. However, for the other three seasons, a beaver's life is more like that of a household dog.

 ## Moose Mating Season

For most creatures in the Adirondacks, autumn is the time to prepare for the coming winter. Squirrels, mice, beavers, and several other rodents focus their attention on adding to their caches of food. Deer, bears, and raccoons actively glean the last berries from bushes and scour the forest floor for any remaining cherries or beechnuts that typically drop during the latter part of this month. Birds, likewise, are solely engaged in developing as much fat as possible to help insulate them against the coming cold or to fuel their eventual migration. For the moose, however, early autumn is the time preparations for winter are halted, due to the reproductive urge that now dominates their life.

From late spring and throughout the summer, the moose spends much of its time quietly wallowing in the waters along remote lake shores or among the pond lilies of a deep marsh. Such shallow aquatic settings provide it with the bulk of its food from June to early September and enable this massive antlered mammal to attain its maximum yearly weight.

It is also in these watery areas that the moose finds relief from the heat of midsummer. Because it is well-adapted for a life in a sub-arctic region, the moose becomes uncomfortably warm when the temperature climbs into the upper 70's. Standing shoulder deep in water also provides relief from the swarms of deer flies, mosquitoes, and black flies that plague northern climates.

With the arrival of autumn weather, and the passing of both insects and aquatic vegetation, the moose becomes much more of a land dweller. Since this time of year marks the onset of their rutting season, moose also begin to travel overland searching for potential mates. This wanderlust is especially intense in healthy adult males, who can cover vast distances when looking for receptive females.

In Canada and Alaska, where there is a sizeable moose population, the bulls only need to cover one or two dozen miles during the rut, since they can repeatedly meet up with enough females to keep them occupied for the duration of this four to six week season.

Both scent and sound are the two means employed by moose to locate each other at this time of year. Odors emitted by unbred cows produce a scent trail that a bull will readily follow upon crossing it. Bulls also give off a scent that helps alert any cow in that area to their presence. Both sexes also produce a mating call which enables two individuals on the prowl for a reproductive experience to home in on each other should they happen to be nearby.

In the Adirondacks, the moose population is currently low. As a result, these long-legged giants are forced to travel far and wide in their often unsuccessful search for mates, with bulls often covering as much as 100 to 200 miles of ground. Because they are continuously on the move, moose sightings increase during late September and for much of October.

With the onset of the rut, the personality of the moose also changes. Ordinarily this behemoth is quite shy and will trot away from a human when approached. Now, however, the bulls are far more interested in locating and pursuing cows than in evading people. Bulls that have been frustrated in their attempts to mate, especially due to larger, more dominant bulls in their immediate area, may charge anything that happens to get in their way.

While caution should always be used when in the vicinity of any wild animal, extra care should be exercised if you happen to cross the path of a thousand pound moose during its mating season. While the chances of encountering a moose in the Adirondacks are low, the moose population is on the rise and is anticipated to continue growing for years to come. While September is the time for enjoying the spectacle of autumn colors, it is also the time when a chance sighting of a moose could add immeasurably to the splendor of a fall landscape.

The Spectacle of Fall Foliage

Throughout most of the Adirondacks, the last week of September and the first week of October are known for their magnificent displays of fall foliage. What starts out around Labor Day with a few isolated trees developing reddish-orange tints, now culminates with a spectacle of color that is as beautiful as any occurrence in the natural world.

Triggered by the invasion of cooler air from Canada and a rapidly dwindling amount of daylight, the trees during September prepare to enter a dormant state that will carry them through the long winter season.

The gradual reduction in the amount of moisture in a tree's woody tissues is one of its first steps in preparing for winter. This prevents ice crystals from forming in its cells, and minimizes the danger associated with the expanding effect of freezing water. As the sap slowly leaves the trunk, the conditions for the continued production of chlorophyll in the leaves deteriorates. Chlorophyll is the green chemical that is essential for changing the sun's energy into useful food in plants.

Along with chlorophyll, there are additional substances in the leaves that help trees utilize the sun's rays, such as *carotene* and *xanthophyll*, which are present in leaves throughout the summer. Xanthophyll is a yellow colored compound, while carotene is orange. However, because of their relatively low concentration compared to chlorophyll, the impact of these two chemicals on the color of a leaf during the summer is minimal. Both of these substances are also less sensitive to changes in the moisture level and temperatures in the leaf compared to chlorophyll. As a result, when trees begin to slow their functions in September, it is the

140

chlorophyll that is the first to disappear, leaving these other two chemicals to color the leaves. Chlorophyll also breaks down rapidly as the amount of daylight diminishes. Many experts believe that this is the primary cause for its disappearance in the fall.

The relative amount of carotene and xanthophyll in the leaves of different trees is one reason for the different autumn colors. Maples, for instance, usually show a greater amount of orange, while cherry and poplar trees show much more yellow.

As cooler temperatures become the rule rather than the exception, many leaves produce another chemical called *anthocyanin*. This substance is used by the foliage to convert some of the sun's rays into heat in order to maintain a temperature favorable for photosynthesis. It also causes a reddish to purple color to appear in leaves.

Auxin is another chemical that is contained in leaves, and although it does not provide any color to the foliage, it does play a significant role in both summer and autumn. There is a special row of cells at the base of a leaf's stem, called the *abscission layer*. Throughout the summer, a certain level of auxin causes this layer of cells to firmly connect the stem to the twig. During periods of strong wind, a twig is more likely to break apart from a branch, taking several leaves along with it, than is a single leaf being pulled from its twig. Changing levels of auxin cause the abscission layer to weaken. Eventually, the mere weight of the leaf is enough to pull it from the twig and send it falling to the ground. The abscission layer then forms a protective covering of cork over the spot on the twig where the stem was attached. This helps seal in the limited amount of moisture that still remains. Cold air tends to be very dry, and dehydration is a plant's biggest problem in winter.

In some trees, especially young beech, auxin levels do not vary appreciably as the leaf dies. Even though the abscission layer still forms a covering of cork between the stem and twig, these cells do not weaken. As a result, they continue to hold the leaf in place until early winter.

There are many factors governing the time that leaves turn color, what shades and hues they will turn, and when they will finally fall to the ground. Whether one is aware of these factors or not, Nature's autumn spectacle is a feast for the eyes that thrills local residents and draws thousands to the area annually.

The Woolly Bear Caterpillar

Over the next several weeks, as autumn begins to tighten its grip on the region, the number of insects will be dramatically reduced. The cool daytime temperatures and frequent nightly frosts kill many bugs and cause most of the others to enter a sheltered place where they will spend the next six to eight months.

One bug that is quite tolerant of the cold and stays active longer than most is the larvae of the isabella tiger moth. This common caterpillar is easily recognized by its inch-long body covered with dense black and reddish-brown hair. This insulating layer of fur-like matter enables it to withstand cooler temperatures and has earned it the name the woolly bear caterpillar.

After hatching from a tiny egg in midsummer, the woolly bear spends all of its time among the blades of overgrown grass and the leaves of unmowed weeds. There it feasts on the foliage of plantain, a common weed of lawns, fields, and roadsides. Because of its small size and preference for staying hidden, woolly caterpillars are not commonly seen before the first hard frost. However, as the autumn foliage nears its peak, they abandon their feeding area to search for a place in which to pass the winter. Unlike most caterpillars, woolly bears will travel a fair distance before settling on a wintering site. A pile of dead leaves, windblown paper that has accumulated along an old fence, or a mound of dried grass and dead brush are favored burrowing spots, offering the best protection against the intense cold soon to come.

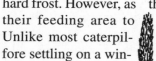
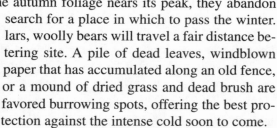

In its travels, the woolly bear is occasionally forced to undulate its way across a sidewalk, driveway, or road. Such movements through open places allow it to be easily seen by humans, as well as by birds and other bug eaters. The dense covering of hair that helps protect it from the cold now aids in preventing it from being eaten by these predators. Most bug eaters do not like to consume such fur-covered insects and will typically leave this caterpillar alone.

The skunk is one of the woolly bear's few natural enemies, grabbing hold of one whenever it can. Before eating them the skunk rolls them around on the ground with its front paws in order to dislodge their woolly coat. Once this has been rubbed off, the skunk is quick to gobble them down.

In the spring, the woolly bear is one of the first ground-dwelling invertebrates to emerge from its dormancy. By mid-April, it can be seen crossing a roadway or sidewalk in an attempt to locate a lawn or field that has scattered clumps of plantain. There it resumes its feeding, and by late spring is ready to spin a cocoon. The process of transforming into an adult usually takes about two weeks.

The isabella tiger moth is not the only insect to have a hairy larval stage. The caterpillars of other species of tiger moths also possess a coat of fur. Like the woolly bear, the lives of these other tiger moth larvae are usually tied to a specific plant or plant group. In the Adirondacks, there are woolly caterpillars that live on dogbane, a common plant of fields and roadsides, and milkweed. Other species occur in wooded areas and live on the leaves of particular types of trees.

Since colonial times, the woolly caterpillars have been used in long-range weather forecasting. Many folklore enthusiasts believe that a dense coat of fur on this bug is a sure sign of a hard winter. But people attempting to gain some insight into the forthcoming weather often fail to take individual differences among the various species into consideration. For instance, the hair on the caterpillar of the tiger moth associated with poplar trees is naturally denser and longer than the hairs covering the caterpillar species dependent upon milkweed. Some people maintain that it is only the larvae of the isabella tiger moth that should be examined for weather prognostication.

Over the next several weeks these insects will be coming out to traverse roads and navigate sidewalks and driveways. You might want to examine one or more for yourself to see what Mother Nature has in store for us this coming winter season.

OCTOBER

The Spawning Brook Trout

To sportsmen, October means hunting season, not fishing. Yet October is when the number one sport fish of the Adirondack backcountry, the brook trout, spawns.

Ordinarily it is very difficult to determine the sex of any fish without first cutting it open. As spawning time nears, however, brook trout develop different features that distinguish the male from the female. The males' dark color brightens noticeably, along with the white and reddish speckles covering their sides and lower jaw hooks, while their back becomes more arched. The females take on a more greenish-silvery appearance, while their sides swell with the developing egg masses inside them.

At the end of September these fish, with their pinkish bellies and slightly forked tails, migrate upstream to suitable spawning sites. As with most members of the salmon and trout family, the brook trout favors shallow streams with a gravel bottom in which to deposit its eggs.

As the swirling water cascades over rocks and stones, oxygen bubbles mix with it. This oxygen rich water is needed by the embryos enclosed in the eggs as they lie among the gravel throughout winter and early spring. The gravel also helps hold the eggs in place, preventing them from being swept downstream, as they would be in sections where the stream bed is covered with sand or silt.

Although gravel helps hold the eggs secure, the female will also excavate a shallow nest to ensure they aren't carried downstream by the current. With her body pointing upstream and lying sideways, she begins to rapidly vibrate her tail fin back and forth, moving away the small stones and pebbles that cover the stream bottom. As she does this, her front pectoral and pelvic fins move in a manner that stabilizes her and prevents her from moving forward.

Once the depression is made, the male swims to the nest alongside the female as the spawning process begins. The female deposits her mass of soft, rounded eggs while the male engulfs them in a cloud of sperm. Although this act lasts for only a few seconds, up to a thousand eggs are released into the nest and fertilized. Immediately afterward, the female swims upstream and begins to kick gravel back onto the nest to cover as many of the eggs as possible.

In cases involving large, healthy trout, a female may produce more eggs than can be laid at a single time. When this happens trout spawn a second time. After the first nest is covered, a new nest is begun a short distance upstream. There the remaining eggs are laid, fertilized, and covered.

Brook trout, like nesting birds, spawn throughout autumn. A multitude of factors, such as water temperature, water chemistry, and the strength of the current affect when a brook trout will lay its eggs. According to Leo Demong, a biologist who specializes in the study of rearing brook trout, *photoperiodism*, or a dependence upon a specific amount of daylight, is the primary underlying factor. As a result, the brook trout spawns at roughly the same time in the same brook each year, despite wide variations in other environmental factors.

If you plan to hike past a clear, small, babbling brook this week or next, look to see if you can observe a brook trout swimming about a circular depression in the gravel bottom. Perhaps spawning might have already occurred there, or it may happen right in front of you.

The Time for Bats to Hibernate

While it will be another month before raccoons, skunks, and bears crawl into their dens and begin their long period of sleep, one group of Adirondack mammals are already entering hibernation. From Labor Day to Election Day, most of the bats that populate the region in summer travel to caves cut deep into the ground, where they will pass the next five to seven months.

As the mercury drops, so does the population of beetles, flies, mosquitoes, and moths upon which the bats feed. As a result, they are forced to take measures to ensure their survival until feeding becomes favorable again. They adapt by gorging themselves on the abundant flying insects that are found between May and September. By consuming nearly half their weight in insects, bats develop a substantial layer of fat over the course of the summer. By mid-September, increasing numbers of bats accumulate enough weight to carry them through spring. At that point bats abandon their nightly foraging trips in favor of resting in the recesses of a cave.

When bats travel to their wintering sites varies greatly, depending upon the species of bat, its sex, and age. Most bats arriving early at the cave entrance are males. Since they do little else but eat in summer, they are the first to fatten up for winter hibernation. The females, however, must take time out from feeding each summer to bear their annual litter of young, which averages only one. Most of the food which the female consumes in spring goes into forming the embryo inside her. A baby bat will be about thirty percent of its mother's weight. After birth, a portion of what she eats produces milk for nursing. As a result, she requires additional feeding time to develop needed fat for winter.

Because young bats are not born until the early summer, and do not start feeding for themselves until late July, they, too, are forced to remain active longer before they are fat enough to enter their wintering caves.

The big brown bat is more tolerant of the cold than other bats. As a result, it refrains from entering its hibernating site until November. This species also differs from its relatives in that it may elect to spend the winter in a partially heated attic or garage, should it find one, rather than in a cave. As long as the temperature in such secluded spots remains above freezing, this bat may remain there throughout the winter.

Although the Adirondacks are not known for their caves, a few deep caverns, especially those around the edges of the Park, satisfy the bat's winter needs. Several abandoned mines, particularly in the Mineville and Lyon Mountain areas, also make for ideal hibernating sites. Some studies have shown that bats will travel a hundred miles or more to reach a cave in which the temperature remains above freezing throughout the winter.

While most bats that populate the Adirondacks retreat into caves and hibernate in winter, three species migrate south. The red bat, silver-haired bat, and hoary bat, which are all uncommon in this region of the state, are sometimes referred to as tree bats, because they hang from branches during the summer days. They seldom enter any type of enclosure to rest, nor do they wedge themselves behind a piece of loose bark or house shutter as other bats are known to do, preferring to rest among clusters of leaves or dense clumps of evergreen needles. From early September through mid-October these bats journey south, as do insect-eating birds. Eventually they end up in the deep South, where conditions are most favorable to them.

For people who dislike having bats fluttering around their heads or flitting about their back porch or deck, October is the month when such concerns diminish substantially. With the exception of a lone big brown bat, which may remain active until sometime around Election Day, the meadows, forests, and lakes finally become free of these beneficial insect eaters during this stage of autumn.

The Great Goose Migration

Once the autumn peak is past, flocks of geese begin to be regularly seen flying over the Adirondacks on their way south. Although the first flock of the fall season can occur in late September, it is not until around Columbus Day that the majority of these birds pass through the region. By Halloween, their frequency diminishes until the last stragglers finally move through during the middle part of November.

Since their honking cries carry beyond a half mile, flocks of geese are usually heard before they are seen. When outdoors on a pleasant, mid-autumn day, most folks instinctively look up to watch for them when they hear their calls.

Geese are also easily recognized in the air by their V-shaped formation. While the two lines flaring out behind the leader are seldom equal in length and the straightness of their ranks fluctuates, there is one characteristic that geese in flight always maintain. The heads and bodies of the trailing birds are always placed directly behind the wing tip of the preceding bird.

Because of their large size, geese encounter a fair amount of air resistance when they fly. In order to minimize this drag, each goose positions itself to take full advantage of the forward turbulence created by the bird in front, very much like cyclists in a bike race. A good competitor will always attempt to reduce his drag as much as possible by pulling up tight behind the individual in front of him. For a goose, this point of maximum pull is located just off the wing tip of the bird in front, rather than to its rear.

Since the goose leading the formation is confronted with the greatest amount of air resistance, flying in this spot requires a greater expenditure of energy. Consequently, after serving as the leader for a minute or two, it is quick to drop back in the flock and let another break trail.

In order to cover the greatest amount of distance with the least amount of effort, geese, like all birds, migrate only when there is a favorable wind. Although the air may appear calm at ground level, the presence of one or more flocks of geese overhead usually indicates a breeze aloft from the north. During times when cold high pressure is ushered into the region by strong northerly gales, geese are likely to remain in flight for the entire day.

A flock that takes full advantage of such a weather system can travel 400 to 500 miles before flying out of these conditions. Should a breeze begin to pick up from the south, geese are quick to find a suitable location in which to wait for better flying weather. Occasionally, it can be several days before a headwind dies and a tailwind begins to pick up.

Although geese are associated with water, these feisty creatures frequently forage on land. Freshly harvested corn or potato fields are favored stopover spots, as are other large, open settings containing a ready supply of fruits, berries, tubers, or seeds. Because of the very limited number of agricultural areas in the Adirondacks, most geese select migration routes away from this mountainous region.

The elevation of the Adirondacks also discourages many geese from crossing the high peaks. The bulk of geese that reach northern New York usually follow the Champlain Valley to the Hudson Valley, or travel up the St. Lawrence to Lake Ontario. From there they make their way to the Finger Lakes, where some Canada Geese spend the winter.

The sight and sound of passing flocks of Canada Geese are as much a part of autumn in the Northeast as are the spectacle of the fall foliage and the fragrance of fresh pressed cider. However, in the Adirondacks, the number of human visitors that will cross the region this weekend will probably exceed that of these honking giants.

The Jumping Mice

With each passing week of autumn, more and more creatures retreat into a state of dormancy. Nearly all the invertebrates that exist in the Adirondacks have already tucked themselves away into some protected spot, or entered into an inactive stage that will last for the next seven to eight months. Turtles, snakes, frogs, and salamanders become quite lethargic in response to cooler weather and soon will withdraw into their own period of hibernation.

Of the various mammals that hibernate to survive the North Country winter, the jumping mice are among the first to enter dormancy. Despite the inevitable spells of pleasant Indian summer weather that occur through the end of this month, these rodents with their lengthy tails are known to retreat to their underground nest around the time of Columbus Day. There they sleep away the next half of the year.

Like the deer and white-footed mouse, and numerous species of voles, jumping mice are extremely common. In the Adirondacks there are two species of these prolific creatures: the woodland jumping mouse, which, as

149

its name implies, resides in the forested areas, and the meadow jumping mouse, which thrives in overgrown fields, along the brushy shores of marshes and ponds, and near forest edges.

Despite their number, jumping mice, like many of their relatives, are not easy to observe. Being nocturnal, these small mammals seldom venture from their subterranean retreats while light remains to make them visible. Sometimes a jumping mouse can be spotted straying into the headlights of a car as it crosses a road or ventures into a clearing on a moonlit night. However, the dark fur of a jumping mouse effectively conceals it once it again enters the shadows of the underbrush.

While both of these species forage primarily on the ground, they can also be observed in shrubs or small trees harvesting a crop of ripening berries or fruits. An assortment of fallen plant seeds, various types of leaves, and several ground dwelling bugs are the staple items in the diet of these creatures, but they will also paw through the layer of dead matter lining the ground in an attempt to uncover and consume the white fungal threads that permeate it.

Unlike other mice and most other rodents, jumping mice do not cache food away. Instead, they develop a layer of fat throughout the summer and early autumn which sustains them during their winter dormancy. Since jumping mice experience a drastic reduction in their overall metabolism, the rate at which they burn food drops substantially, and their need for nourishment diminishes correspondingly.

When sources of food are limited or when competition for it is excessive, a jumping mouse may be unable to form an adequate layer of fat. As a result, it will remain active for a longer span of time in October in an attempt to make up the difference. A jumping mouse can also awaken from its hibernation earlier in the spring if its fat reserve becomes exhausted before mid-April, when it traditionally emerges from its burrow. But sometimes they simply die in their nest during the winter should the fat that fuels their system become depleted.

With the exception of a few ecologists or wildlife biologists investigating the natural history of small mammals, the gradual reduction and eventual disappearance of jumping mice from the forests and fields goes unnoticed by humans. However, their absence is surely felt by the ermine, fox, bobcat, owl, fisher, and other predators. For such carnivores, this time of autumn marks the beginning of the season when the quantity of available game starts its long and unwelcome decline.

The Highly Visible Red Squirrel

While many different mammals exist in the Adirondacks, none seems to maintain such a conspicuous profile as the red squirrel. With its occasional chatter and its boldness around human dwellings, especially in its persistent visits to bird feeders, the red squirrel is difficult to overlook.

During the autumn, particularly in October, the red squirrel's food gathering activity increases, as it does in most other rodents. Although this familiar rusty-tan colored packrat feeds on a variety of items, its main source of nourishment comes from the tiny seeds contained in the woody cones of evergreen trees. With its set of sharp incisors, the red squirrel easily gnaws through the cone's tough protective exterior. While evergreen seeds are not as large as the triangular nuts of the beech or the winged helicopter seeds of the sugar maple, they contain a fair amount of nutrients and, when eaten in large quantities, are adequate to meet the needs of this small rodent.

To ensure that all of its seeds remain enclosed in the cone prior to eating, the red squirrel harvests them well before they open. Throughout autumn, it spends much of its time cutting down the "green" cones of the pines, spruces, balsam fir, cedar, and hemlock and then letting them drop to the ground. (It takes a cone two growing seasons to develop completely. During the summer of its second year, the cone dries while still attached to the twig. It then opens to release its seeds. After all the seeds have been dispersed, the open cone eventually drops from the tree.)

After several dozen unopened cones have been cut loose from the upper twigs, the red squirrel gathers them up and carries them to a subterranean chamber for storage. Since the conditions underground never get too warm or dry, the cones placed there never open to lose their tiny seeds.

During times when cones are abundant, the squirrel stores away more food than it can use in winter. Occasionally, its storage chamber may become filled, in which case it piles its collected cones in a protected place on the surface of the forest floor.

When it comes time for a winter meal, the red squirrel will remove a cone from its natural refrigerator and proceed to a favored dining spot. Such places are easily recognized by the mound of cone fragments that litter the ground around them. A stump, the end of a downed log, or a spot near the base of a large tree are typical locations where a red squirrel eats its cones.

Along with cones, the red squirrel caches other edibles it encounters when foraging, such as wild black cherries and other fruits, as well as mushrooms. In order to reduce spoilage in items having a high water content, the little forager often places them in a spot exposed to the sun. In places where wild apples occur, a red squirrel will usually wedge the ripened fruit in a crotch of the trunk, or on a forked branch where it can dry. It also places mushrooms on the outer boughs of evergreens where the sun can bake the moisture from them before they are tucked away for use in winter.

Sunflower seeds are another favored item in the diet of red squirrels. In places with well-stocked bird feeders, this resourceful creature will go to great lengths to get its fair share of human handouts. During autumn, when its drive to accumulate food is especially strong, it can make a nuisance of itself around bird feeders.

Like a miser hoarding all the money he can get, the red squirrel continues to take seeds from a feeder, rather than dipping into its own stockpile of stored food when the weather turns cold. The only difference is that the red squirrel will visit a feeder for several hours a day in winter, compared to its marathon assaults on the feeders during October.

Active Mice

For most Adirondack rodents, autumn is both a time of harvest and the season to prepare a shelter for the coming winter. Chipmunks, for example, are currently busy either enlarging a storage chamber in their burrow to accommodate the recently fallen crop of beechnuts, or picking up the remaining maple keys and other tree seeds from the forest floor. The red squirrel and beaver are also actively involved with the chores of winterizing their homes and setting in their store of food.

For the mice that populate the Adirondacks, the routine of autumn is little different from that experienced by most other rodents. Each day, around sunset, these small nocturnal animals begin the task of searching for food. Any items located in the early evening are eaten on the spot. Fallen tree seeds, dried fruits, berries that have dropped to the ground, already hibernating bugs, and clusters of dormant insect eggs compose the bulk of their diet. Along with their meal at dusk, mice also consume food throughout the night, especially at this time of year. In this way these small furry creatures are able to develop a layer of fat before winter sets in. This helps insulate them against the cold, and provides a potential source of nourishment should their caches of food run low or become exhausted.

After satisfying their appetite, mice continue to forage throughout the night, transporting what they find to a protective site for use in winter. Such food deposits are likely to be located in places that offer easy access when a deep blanket of snow covers the ground. Crevices beneath rocks, holes under fallen logs, cavities in standing tree trunks, and soft soil under uprooted trees are common food cache sites. Mice, like chipmunks, have internal cheek pouches that enable them to carry a full meal of food to their cache in a single trip.

Along with obtaining a food supply, mice throughout the autumn also prepare a number of nests that can shelter them from winter's harshness. This allows them to quickly relocate during the dead of winter should one of their homes be destroyed. These retreats are usually oval in shape and average ten inches in length. The exterior tends to be made of interwoven pieces of grass and hair. The bulk of the nest, however, is generally made of shredded bits of dried leaves and cushiony mosses, lined with feathers or the downy seeds of milkweed.

Any place that affords protection from wind, rain, and dripping water is likely to be selected as a site for a nest. These include hollow logs, holes in trees, cracks between rocks, or depressions beneath dense mounds of brush. In places with high mouse populations, most available nesting sites can already be taken. In such cases, mice are forced to seek shelter in a shed or barn, between the walls of a house, or in a seldom used closet.

Contrary to a popular notion, mice do not restrict

153

their activity to the ground, for they are good climbers. Their sharp claws enable them to easily cling to rough surfaces, such as tree bark, and their long tail helps them balance as they scamper across a narrow twig or ascend a steep limb. Their skill at scaling objects allows them access to sheltered areas well off the ground, including attics or rafter spaces. Additionally, their ability to squeeze through small openings, such as the narrow gap between a floor and a pantry closet door, enables them to get into places that appear closed to intruders.

Because mice breed continuously throughout the spring, summer, and early autumn, their population tends to reach a peak during this time. Additionally, their urge to construct nests during the fall leads these unwanted visitors into cottages, camps, and homes as winter approaches.

The presence of a pet cat can have a definite impact on the number of mice in and around your house. However, if you are without such protection, a mouse trap can eliminate this temporary problem. Since mice use their sense of smell to locate food, it is important to bait such traps with a substance that will provide a lasting aroma. While cheese has long been considered to be the ideal bait, peanut butter is far more effective in luring a mouse to a particular spot.

As autumn wanes, and cold, snowy weather becomes more commonplace, mice settle into their wintertime routine. Around Thanksgiving, their desire to establish a new nest dwindles, as does the urge to explore their surroundings. If a mouse has not constructed some type of shelter in your house by that time, the chances are slim that you will see one until mid-spring, when their population begins to once more rise.

The Sound of the Shrews

It doesn't take long after an autumn rain for the layer of freshly fallen foliage to become dry and crisp. A day or two of sun, wind, warm temperatures, and low humidity is all that is needed to change a soggy carpet of downed leaves into a bed of loose crunchy matter that rustles with the slightest disturbance. Such conditions in mid-autumn can convert a silent forest into a rather noisy woodland.

During such weather, the presence of any creature moving about on the ground in a deciduous woodland is quickly revealed. Chipmunks and red squirrels can be heard a good distance away as they scamper about foraging for food and transporting collected items back to their favored cache site. Grouse also make their presence known as they walk across this crispy carpet or scratch through it in search of fallen seeds or dormant insects wintering beneath it. Even mice and voles, which ordinarily go undetected as they move about the forest floor, disturb the dried leaves enough to produce an easily noticed noise.

Despite their incredibly small size, shrews likewise expose their presence during dry spells in mid-autumn as they nose their way over, under, around, and through the layer of shriveled, brown, brittle leaves. Among the most abundant mammals within the Adirondacks, these tiny, long-nosed creatures, which are smaller than mice, are not commonly seen. Typically, shrews reside under the layer of leaf litter, dead twigs, rotting logs, and fallen bark that accumulates on the ground in wooded areas.

During most of the year, dampness permeates this layer of organic debris blanketing the forest floor. It is further compacted by the weight of the usually heavy winter snow, making it much less fluffy and crunchy. Consequently, with the exception of autumn, shrews produce very little, if any, perceptible disturbance as they travel about, checking the nooks and crannies among moss-covered rocks, uprooted trees, and decaying stumps. This allows shrews to conduct their ceaseless search for food without being noticed by a nearby human.

Although they are more active in the late afternoon and throughout the evening, their high demand for food causes shrews to also go on the prowl for food during the day. Their metabolism is among the highest of any mammal, and some researchers have noted various shrews consuming well over their own weight in food per day.

Ground dwelling invertebrates, such as soil insects, worms, millipedes, centipedes, slugs, and spiders, compose the main items of their diet. Beginning in autumn, as the number of active bugs dwindle, shrews start to search more among the

fallen leaves and other forest litter for dormant invertebrates, clusters of wintering eggs, larvae, and pupas, as well as the remains of adults that have already reproduced and succumbed to the cold.

Shrews also attack larger animals they happen to encounter as they move about the forest floor. Mice, voles, ground nesting birds such as sparrows and juncos, and even immature chipmunks are occasional victims of these fierce, gray predators.

One very common species of shrew in the Adirondacks is the short-tailed shrew, which relies on venom for killing such small mammals. Like poisonous reptiles, it introduces a toxic fluid into the body of its intended prey when biting it. After the encounter, the shrew simply follows the scent trail of the rapidly dying victim in order to recover the carcass. A slain mouse or chipmunk can contain enough food for an entire day or more.

Like hounds, shrews also have a very well developed sense of smell. Because they spend so much of their time beneath the layer of dead leaves, or in shallow subterranean tunnels where light is limited or non-existent, shrews do not rely on their vision. As a result, their eyes are quite small and beady. Though their sense of hearing is also only fair, their sense of touch is most acute. Shrews, like mice and many other wild creatures, have a number of sensory hairs extending from the sides of their snout. These are known as *vibrissae,* and function as feelers, providing shrews with information on the environment immediately in front of them, such as the layer of leaf litter you might hear them rustle through when you are out hiking this time of year.

The Hornet's Nest

Shortly after Columbus Day, as the last of the leaves begin to drop, the summer homes of many creatures finally become unveiled. Among the branches of deciduous trees and shrubs, a wide variety of birds and insects place their nests. These generally remain well hidden throughout the late spring and summer, even when placed directly over a sidewalk, next to a well-trodden path, or alongside a driveway.

The largest structure located in the branches of broad-leaf trees, which usually goes unnoticed until the surrounding foliage falls, is the nest of the bald-faced hornet. This egg-shaped, gray colored structure measures over a foot in length and in diameter at its widest point. Usually it is fashioned around the end of one or more twigs, and located anywhere from four to twenty five feet above the forest floor. Although often labeled as a bee hive, only the bald-faced hornet erects such a nest. Wild honey bees typically locate their nest in the shelter of a hollow tree, or in the recesses of some other cavity close to the ground.

The nest of the bald-faced hornet is started by a single, fertilized queen during mid-spring. After selecting a suitable site, the queen constructs a dozen or so papery cells that will house her first eggs and larvae. Once completed, this small cluster of cells is enveloped in a thin covering made of the same paper-like substance.

After the eggs are laid it takes nearly a month until they develop into adults. The first of the hornets produced by the queen are sterile females, better known as workers. These quickly assume the tasks of building more cells and tending to the needs of the queen and the rapidly growing larvae. As summer passes, the population of the nest swells, and by Labor Day can number into the thousands. In order to accommodate all of these hornets, the nest is enlarged throughout the summer until, by the end of the season, it has reached its peak size.

Like yellow jackets and other types of wasps, the bald-faced hornet makes its nest out of a material similar to papier-mache. When it comes time to work on its shelter, the hornet first locates a source of suitable plant fiber, such as a piece of partially rooted wood. It then bites off a mouthful and thoroughly chews the fibrous matter while mixing it with its saliva. Upon returning to its nest, the hornet then smears this pulpy substance into a thin sheet which dries to form a unique layer of paper.

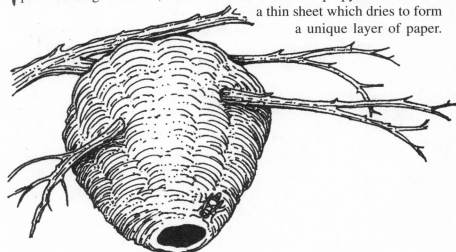

Repeated trips by many workers to sources of plant fibers are made throughout the summer, resulting in a nest composed of multiple tiers of cells enclosed by a dense protective covering.

The size and shape of a wasp nest, along with its general location, can
be used as a means of identifying the occupants. Yellow jackets always
construct their papier-mache house in a cavity below ground. Members of
the group known as polistes wasps limit their nest to a single row of cells
and never enclose them with a papery covering. These structures are commonly attached to the back of house shutters, under eaves, or to a rafter in
a garage or shed. The potter wasp, like the bald-faced hornet, fashions a
papery covering around its nursery; however, the entire structure is seldom
larger than a golf ball, and usually the shape of a rounded clay pot.

Unlike the bee hive, a wasp nest is not used to store honey, nor is it
occupied in winter. As the first weeks of October bring freezing temperatures, all of the workers in the colony die. Only the queens that develop at
the end of the summer from special eggs survive the winter, and they never
remain in the nest past mid-September. The males, or drones, also abandon
the nest, along with the recently formed queens in order to mate with them.
Shortly after breeding, the drones die, and the fertilized females seek out a
sheltered spot, often in a hole under ground, where they pass the next six or
seven months.

When the leaves have fallen in mid-October, the totally deserted nest
of the bald-faced hornet hangs from the bare branches. Although I know
that this uniquely sculptured structure no longer contains any live hornets
by this time of year, I always wait until late November or December before
attempting to handle one, as I have an irrational fear of meeting up with
these short-tempered insects.

NOVEMBER

The Loon Migration

As winter sets in during mid-November, the last of the summer birds readies for migration south. The loon, which commonly inhabits the Adirondacks' many lakes and ponds, lingers until ice starts to form over its pristine northern home. A thick deposit of insulating fat on its underside, and a dense covering of plumage, allows the loon to sit continuously in near freezing water without becoming excessively chilled.

Even when the small fish it eats move into deeper water, the loon has little difficulty in catching a meal at this time of year. Its ability to dive to great depths lets it find food as long as the surface remains free of ice. But once an icy barrier cuts the loon off from its underwater food supply, the time arrives to either leave or perish.

Not all loons wait until November to migrate; some abandon the North Country during the late summer. Once the loon chick is able to fend for itself, the family dissolves, and the parents begin to travel outside the boundaries of their spring-summer breeding territory. Instead of simply venturing off on a local excursion, some loons extend their flight and migrate early. Most adults, though, do not start their journey south until this month.

As a loon visits other ponds, it usually encounters birds that occupied neighboring bodies of water. Although the loon, with its unmistakable wailing cry, is not noted for existing in flocks, small, loosely-knit groups of loons sometimes form several weeks prior to their departure from the region.

Loon chicks are slow to learn to fly. Since swimming and diving are more important to them in acquiring food and escaping from enemies, these

159

are the skills that are most quickly developed. It is not until mid- to late September that young loons leave the surface of the water for the first time.

Occasionally, a pair of loons get a slow start in nesting during the spring, causing their eggs to hatch much later than normal. These late season chicks may not develop the ability to pull their heavy bodies out of the water until early November, and can have a difficult time making the journey south.

Loons spend the winter on the open ocean, off the coast of the southern and mid-Atlantic states. Even though the seas offshore can be quite rough, loons can weather most turbulent waters. Young birds have the most trouble adjusting to such difficult conditions, especially during severe storms. As a result, the majority of juvenile loons die before reaching adulthood at the age of three.

Although the loon population declined greatly several decades ago, their numbers are now slowly increasing. This indicates that enough young birds are surviving the rigors of their existence to fill the void left by the adults that have perished, reclaiming their ancestors' bodies of water.

If you plan on spending time this winter along the sandy beaches of the south, you might want to scan the surf with a good pair of binoculars to see if you can spot a small flock of the birds that have come to symbolize the Adirondack wilderness.

Downy Woodpecker Activity

While the warm breezes of spring are months away, in November some birds are already taking the first step in their breeding process. Male and female mallards, like most other forms of waterfowl, often establish a pair bond during the fall. While this interaction may not keep them together during migration or when they are on their wintering grounds, it does cause them to seek each other out when mating season approaches in the late winter and early spring.

The downy woodpecker's activities in November also indicate they are forming a pair bond for the coming mating season early next year. For most of the autumn these birds, the smallest woodpeckers in North America, are quite solitary. Each moves about the forest independently looking for ripe berries that have fallen to the ground, or bugs living under tree bark.

By early November, the downy begins to associate more and more with a member of the opposite sex. The two may even perform several rituals normally associated only with their mating behavior. As is the case with the mallards, however, they often again part company as winter begins to set in.

If you hang suet or peanut butter outside and frequently get downy woodpeckers coming to eat, you will notice that these black and white creatures are more likely during November to show up in pairs, each of them lured there by the presence of a potential mate.

Along with forming a pair bond with another of its kind, this short, tough-billed bird also excavates its nighttime roosting cavity during this month. Around Halloween, the downy, like other woodpeckers, develops the urge to spend nights inside the shelter of a tree cavity. Throughout the summer and early autumn, it simply perches on a tree limb next to the trunk at sunset and rests until the following morning. However, as the nights become colder, a shelter is sought to protect it from cold temperatures and chill winds.

Tall, dead trees or live trunks with partially rotted centers are commonly selected as roosting sites. One researcher has noted that the downy takes about a week, working off and on, to chisel and chip the small, rounded entrance hole, along with a suitable sized chamber within the trunk. Around sunset each evening the downy will return to that spot, enter the hole, fluff up its plumage, then settle down for the night.

Because of the amount of time they spend together during November, a pair of downies is likely to excavate their roosting cavity in the same general vicinity. Yet, because they do not lay claim to any particular territory, these birds will not exclude other downies from establishing roosting sites nearby. In fact, one ornithologist discovered two females roosting in separate cavities of the same tree.

Although tolerant of other downies, this bird will become quite aggressive toward any other woodpecker that gets too close to its nightly retreat. The hairy woodpecker, which is nearly identical in appearance to the downy except for its size, has been known to enlarge the entrance and cavity so as to accommodate its larger body, and then slip into this roost before the downy returns for the night.

In the forests of the Adirondack Park, the abundance of dead, standing timber provides the woodpeckers with numerous places to excavate their roosting cavity. As a result, there is little competition for these hollow shelters, compared to other regions. It is in places in which trees are periodically harvested, thereby eliminating unhealthy or partially rotted stands of timber, that the downy is most vulnerable to having its roosting site taken over by another woodpecker. But overall, the ease with which this gentle bird is able to find a suitable tree in the primitive woodlands provides it with that much more time during November to spend with its future mate.

The Deer Rut

To U.S. citizens, Veterans' Day is a time to pay tribute to the many people in uniform who have served throughout our history. In the world of the Adirondacks, however, white-tailed deer know it as the peak of the rut, or breeding season.

Unlike black bears, most birds, and many other creatures whose rut spans a month or more, for white-tailed deer this season lasts only about two weeks. In places with a healthy distribution of bucks and does, it is estimated that over 75 percent of the females are bred during this time frame, starting in early November and peaking around November 11.

As with spawning brook trout, the deer rut occurs each year when daylight dwindles to a particular length, and begins regardless of prolonged periods of unseasonably cold or warm autumn weather.

With November's approach, the personality of the whitetail changes, especially that of the buck. During the summer, deer are gregarious. A doe is often accompanied by her newborn fawns and occasionally by her young of the previous year. The males occupying a given area also spend much of their time together in small herds. During late October, however, they become increasingly intolerant of the presence of other bucks in the immediate area. Encounters between competing males usually result in the two approaching each other with heads held down and pointed antlers angled forward. When they clash, each attempts to outpush the other. In this way the stronger and healthier buck wins the right to control that particular area.

During these battles, the neck of the deer endures tremendous amounts of stress. In order to minimize the risk of injury, the neck muscles swell during the rut to absorb as much of the strain of this type of fighting as possible.

With the onset of rutting season, bucks also travel more. During most of the year, a male whitetail in the Adirondacks roams over approximately one square mile of territory. As breeding time arrives, this expands to over one and a half square miles. The larger and stronger deer are the ones that travel furthest, often venturing into the home range of neighboring bucks. The outcome of the inevitable battle determines if the interloper is free to stay and pursue any doe in heat in that area, or is forced back into his own territory.

Should a buck defeat a neighboring male, it must still frequently return to its traditional home range to safeguard against rival bucks infringing on its right to breed with the does of that area.

When they are not fighting, bucks are continually on the go searching for does in heat. A female in estrus gives off various scents that help attract the buck. This is why bucks trot through the woods at this time of year with their noses held close to the ground, like beagles on the trail of a snowshoe rabbit. A buck following the scent of a doe in heat at this time of year can

163

fail to notice a nearby hiker or hunter and walk directly up to a person in the woods, rather than bounding away before it gets too close.

Traveling across their own territory, venturing into the territory of others, fighting, and being in constant pursuit of does keeps bucks active for most of the day and much of the night. Since mating now takes precedence over even feeding, many bucks lose weight over this two week period. Big bucks can lose from ten to fifteen percent of their body weight This is why most deer killed during late October are heavier and contain more fat than comparable sized bucks shot around Thanksgiving.

It has been said that deer are well aware of the beginning of hunting season, as they tend to change their habits and places which they frequent. Perhaps these graceful creatures do know when it is time for them to lie low. However, some biologists simply attribute this change in behavior to the onset of the rut.

The Porcupine Mating Season

With winter bearing down on the region, Adirondack rodents that do not hibernate are busy preparing for the lean months soon to come. Red and flying squirrels spend much of their time accumulating a cache of cones, seeds, and dried berries, while beavers are assembling the underwater stockpile of limbs and branches that will serve as food when ice covers their watery world. Mice and voles collect a store of assorted items on which they partially rely for nourishment over the next several months. Even muskrats, which are not known as packrats, form small caches of cattail and arrowhead roots with the approach of winter. Only the porcupine does not follow this rule, spending little time getting ready for life during the following season. Because the sharp, barb-tipped quills that cover their bodies and tails are hollow, they act as an excellent covering of insulation, protecting them not only from large woodland predators, but also from winter's bitter cold.

From the time of the last of the falling leaves until new growth sprouts, porcupines feed on the inner bark of certain hardwood

164

and softwood trees, and on hemlock needles. Since these items are abundantly accessible throughout the winter, the porcupine has no real need to spend any of its time during autumn collecting and hoarding food. Instead, like the white-tailed deer, it turns its attention toward mating.

Unlike deer, however, the porcupine's breeding season is not as well synchronized. A female can come into heat any time between late October and the third week of December. Since her estrus period only lasts about ten to twelve hours, the male will attempt to remain with the female almost continuously until she is receptive. If she fails to breed during this brief time, she will re-enter another heat period approximately thirty days later. In addition, shortly before she becomes receptive, she produces a chemical that is mixed in with her urine, advertising the fact that she will soon be ready to breed.

During the fall, the males wander about more, compared to other months. Upon detecting a smell that indicates a female near estrus, the male will attempt to home in on her. In areas abundant with porcupines, the female's scent sometimes lures more than one suitor. In such cases the males will fight one another for the right to breed with her. Although not known as aggressive animals, porcupines can be downright nasty if the need arises. Competing males attempt to bite one another, which can be a serious act of aggression, considering their sharp, chisel-like teeth and their powerful jaw muscles. Because porcupines are not immune to each other's quills, such encounters can also lead to them being severely wounded by their rival's sharp, stiff hairs.

Before mating occurs there is a brief period of courtship. The male performs a "dance" in front of his partner, moving about on three legs while one of the front legs is held up against his lower belly. While dancing, he makes a low-pitched whining sound. The female responds by squirming about on the ground, rubbing her undersides on the forest floor near her potential mate. When the female is ready to breed, she pulls her quills tight against her body so that the male can make contact with her without being impaled.

After mating, the two animals spend up to a day together before drifting apart. But because porcupines confine their travels to limited areas (in winter they may have a home range of less than eight acres), the two can remain within the same immediate area until spring. During periods of intense cold, these normally solitary creatures have been known to share a den or shelter with a neighbor, thereby helping to conserve body warmth.

During such occasions little social interaction occurs between them, and the events of the past November are undoubtedly long forgotten.

The Varying Hare

While the season's first few flakes of snow can appear in the Adirondacks as early as mid-September, it is not until mid-November that enough snow covers the ground to stay for any length of time. Such snowfalls are a delight to both anxious skiers eager to hit the slopes, and big game hunters, who use the powdery blanket to help track their quarry.

Snowfall is also key to the success of the varying hare, which like the landscape undergoes a similar change in color. Triggered by the decreasing daylight, this hare, also known as the snowshoe rabbit, starts its autumn molt in mid-October. Its ears and feet are the first to shed its darker summer hair, to be replaced by its white winter coat. By November, an increasingly greater percentage of its legs and the area around its head turns white, followed by the lower sections of its sides, leaving only its back grayish-brown in color.

Its new coat enables this common prey to blend in with the typical November landscape. Despite the intensity of a late autumn snowstorm, usually some bare ground remains in groves of hemlocks, or beneath the closely spaced boughs of spruce or fir. Conversely, even during an unseasonably mild spell, scattered pockets of snow usually linger in places protected from the sun.

By the second week of December, the transformation is complete, at which time the hare appears pure white, except for some black around the upper fringe of its ears. Along with its long, white guard hairs, which are so effective in camouflaging it against a snowy background, the varying hare also supports a dense layer of light, almond-colored underfur that helps insulate it against winter's cold. In addition, its enlarged hind feet act like snowshoes. This added advantage for traveling across the snow helps it contend with the increased pressure that it experiences from winter predators. With so many animals hibernating and the disappearance of migratory birds, many predators are forced to concentrate prey on this tasty, small game animal.

To further avoid being seen by its natural enemies, the varying hare confines its activities to areas with an entangled mass of underbrush. Alder thickets and conifer swamps, with their dense understory, are favored haunts of this mammal, not only helping to conceal its presence, but enabling it to outmaneuver any predator that should happen to detect it. Places where the forest floor is relatively open, such as mature stands of hardwoods, are seldom visited in winter.

Besides affording cover, evergreen thickets provide the hare with tree buds and conifer needles to eat. Like the white-tailed deer, the varying hare is quite selective as to which types of twigs it will nibble. Maples, birches, willows, and alders are frequently eaten; however, the buds of poplars and the scale-like foliage of cedar are especially preferred. Often a fallen aspen twig may be chewed on until all of the bark has been removed. Unlike a beaver, which is known for stripping the bark from fair-size aspen limbs, the varying hare tends to gnaw only on the smaller branches.

Over the past decade, unseasonably mild autumn weather and the late arrival of snow have created some dangerous background conditions for the varying hare. During such occasions, it restricts its movements until the situation improves. Ordinarily, it does not take very much snow to produce favorable conditions; only a dusting, creating a white woodland scene, is enough to conceal the varying hare. Although foxes, coyotes, bobcats, and other forest predators all have exceptionally keen eyesight, their ability to discern this timid creature from its surroundings diminishes substantially whenever patches of snow blanket the ground.

The Black Bear Retreats for Winter

While the list of creatures that hibernate during winter is quite long, the black bear has come to represent this group above all the others. In the Adirondacks, it is usually around Thanksgiving that these massive mammals begin to settle down for their long winter rest. The females are the first to enter a den, usually beginning their prolonged period of sleep the third or fourth week of November. Males remain active slightly longer, and may not bed down until early December.

While a cave is thought of as the traditional denning site, black bears in the North Country seldom rely on such an opening in a rocky hillside. Almost any place that affords protection from snow, rain, and chilling winter breezes can be used as a den. In the Adirondacks, bears curl up in depressions beneath the upturned roots of a fallen tree. A pile of brush, especially one covered by a large, downed evergreen tree, is also used as a den on occasion, as are crevices between large rocks and cubbies under massive boulders.

The male is less selective about its den than the female. Because the sow bear often has cubs with her, or will be giving birth to a litter during the middle of winter, she ordinarily chooses a place that is as sheltered as possible.

Once it has decided upon a particular spot, the bear often digs a shallow depression in the soil with its powerful front legs. This further protects it from the elements. It may also pull together several handfuls of dried leaves or other soft debris from the ground to serve as bedding material.

After it settles down, the bear usually sleeps until spring. During unusually warm periods of thaw, it may briefly awaken and get up to lumber around for a short distance. This is especially true of the male. A female, however, especially if she has cubs with her, seldom leaves the den no matter how pleasant the midwinter weather.

Because of internal physiological changes, a bear is more than capable of spending the next several months without any food or water. Energy is provided for maintaining its life processes by burning the massive deposit of fat it accumulates prior to hibernating. Water that is produced as waste during respiration and filtered out by the kidneys is reabsorbed back into the blood. This prevents the bear from dehydrating, and allows it to sleep for months at a time without needing to urinate.

Although the bear's life process slows down considerably, this reduction is far less than what occurs in other mammals. In creatures like the woodchuck, jumping mouse, or bat, the amount of metabolic depression is dramatically greater. This is why it is far easier to arouse a bear from its winter sleep than these other creatures. Because hibernation is biologically defined in terms of what these other mammals experience during winter, the bear is not regarded as a true hibernator. Like the raccoon and skunk, it is considered to be only a prolonged sleeper.

Along with denning, embryonic development also begins shortly after Thanksgiving. While bears mate during the late spring and early summer, the embryos formed during this process hardly develop until the female retires into her den. Since it takes up to two months for them to fully develop, it is not until January that they are born.

As the pace of life for people becomes increasingly more hectic with the holiday season approaching, it is often interesting to think of the black bear resting comfortably, and remaining that way for the next four months.

The Ermine

To most people, the term predator conjures up images of large, aggressive creatures feeding on the flesh of slaughtered animals. But, while all predators do possess fierce temperaments, not all of them are large. The ermine is a perfect example. This member of the weasel family is every bit as blood thirsty as any coyote, bobcat, fisher, or bear, but is barely the length of a red squirrel, and only weighs as much as the delicate chipmunk.

Like the lynx, fox, otter, and various other carnivores, the ermine has prominent and pointed canine teeth. These enable it to tear through the hide of thick-skinned animals and rip apart the meat from a freshly killed carcass.

In contrast to its meat-eating relatives, the ermine does not retain its summer color as autumn turns to winter. During early November, long white hairs begin to replace the light chocolate colored fur that covers this elusive creature throughout the warmer months. By Thanksgiving, the ermine is pure white in color, except for a black tip on its rather short tail. This dense white fur, like that of the varying hare, insulates it against the bitter cold and helps conceal its presence. Despite its predatory nature, the ermine occasionally becomes the target of other hunters, such as the fox, coyote, bobcat, fisher, owl, and hawk. Fortunately, its colored coat makes it more difficult for its prey to detect it. Both in summer and winter, the ermine sneaks about the forest floor without being noticed by the small animals upon which it preys.

Mice and voles are the main items in the ermine's diet. Because both of these rodents average one-third the weight of an ermine, a successful kill provides it with a full day's nourishment, while a chipmunk or small ruffed grouse can last an ermine for several days. During late spring and summer, the ermine attacks immature varying hares, which are three to five times its own weight. Although such efforts yield enough food for nearly a week, the ermine seldom relies on a partially eaten carcass for that length of time. After making a kill and feasting on its remains for a while, it is quick to renew its hunt for fresh game.

When there is an abundance of small animals, the ermine often destroys far more creatures than it could ever eat. Should it be overly successful, it will usually drag its excess victims to some suitable nook or cranny for later consumption. Beginning in early December, when the temperature of tiny cubbies existing beneath rotting logs, in rock crevices, or under uprooted trees remains below freezing, a natural refrigeration is created that will last until spring, ensuring that the ermine's cache of meat stays well preserved.

During warmer months, however, any dead game will spoil in a week or be devoured by maggots and other scavenging invertebrates.

In the Adirondacks, the ermine is perhaps the most abundant of the carnivores roaming the forest, meadows, and swamps in search of quarry. Because of its small size, secretive habits, and protective coloration, this dwarf weasel often passes unobserved. However, as snow begins to cover the ground, its presence can be noted by the set of tracks it leaves behind. Most folks who see these imprints, however, usually mistake them for those of a squirrel, as their size is seldom associated with that of a voracious predator.

The Uncommon Gray Squirrel

It is easy to get a false impression of the abundance of a particular animal population by relying on observations made only through a kitchen window or from a car when traveling around a North Country village. Because most wild creatures in the Adirondacks are wary of humans, they avoid places where they are readily exposed to the public's view. Many creatures also favor an existence in an uninhabited wilderness, as opposed to settings which contain numerous human dwellings.

But several animals thrive only in places populated by people, causing their numbers to be overestimated by local residents. At the top of this list is the gray squirrel, which generally limits its range in the Adirondacks to those places where humans maintain bird feeders. In the towns and hamlets within the Blue Line, this chubby, gray rodent with its bushy tail is one of the most observed animals, since it spends much of its time foraging in places that support containers filled with sunflower seeds. It would be unusual to have a well-stocked feeder and not have a few gray squirrels living nearby. However, in the vast expanses of wilderness that cover the majority of land in this region, the gray squirrel is extremely scarce. And in the high elevation forests and dense stands of evergreens, this nemesis of indoor bird watchers is totally absent.

Like many animals that reside in warmer climates, the gray squirrel has a fondness for the hefty seeds of oak and hickory trees, with acorns and hickory nuts being the staple items in its diet. Since neither of these groups of valuable hardwoods are plentiful in the Adirondack deciduous woodlands, most areas in the Park fail to support a gray squirrel population.

171

With their milder weather and longer growing seasons, the Champlain and St. Lawrence Valleys are able to produce a fair number of oaks, clusters of which also exist around the periphery of the Park. Consequently, in these areas the gray squirrel is far more numerous.

Regardless of whether the gray squirrel obtains its food by foraging on natural supplies of food, pilfering birdseed, or raiding bags of garbage, it becomes much less active as winter sets in. On days when the mercury hovers around zero, or when there is an exceptionally low chill factor, the gray squirrel remains in its nest most of the day. Occasionally, it will emerge to make a quick jaunt to a feeder, or to forage around the base of a large oak tree attempting to find a meal. Such excursions occur only after the temperature rises from its early morning low. If these trips prove fruitless, the squirrel will visit one of the caches of food that it assembled earlier in the year.

Unlike other squirrels known for their antisocial behavior, this species is tolerant of its neighbors. During times of bitter cold, grays have been known to congregate in a central nest. By huddling together in the close quarters of a single living chamber, several grays are able to share their body warmth and thereby conserve heat.

Like several other animals, the gray squirrel is prone to a condition known as *melanism*. This causes its fur to be tinted black rather than gray. Such an animal is not a separate species of wildlife; it is just the brunette form of a gray squirrel.

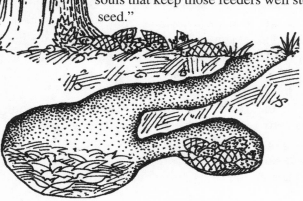

Many gray squirrels can be seen in and around the villages of the Adirondacks because of their relative abundance in such populated areas. However, such a situation would never exist if it were not for the kindhearted souls that keep those feeders well stocked with "squirrel seed."

DECEMBER

The Adaptable Coyote

While the strategies that wildlife employ for surviving a northern winter vary greatly from one creature to another, there is a considerable degree of similarity as to what members of the same species will do during the coming winter. For example, regardless of where they reside, all beavers tend to confine their activities to trips between their family lodge and their underwater food pile just outside the entrance. Likewise, all meadow voles develop the same regular routine of movement about their network of runways existing among the dried and collapsed stalks of grasses and weeds. And the chickadees' method of searching for food is little different from those friendly, black-capped birds that occupy a more temperate setting.

However, for the coyote, winters spent in the heavily forested areas within the Blue Line are entirely different from those passed in more agricultural regions outside the Park. In the pasturelands and open fields of the Champlain and St. Lawrence Valleys, as well as in southern New York State, this wily canine spends the majority of its time in a solitary search for something to eat.

In open areas, the greatest concentrations of food are small game animals, such as cottontail rabbits, woodchucks, mice, voles, and pheasants. Since these creatures are more successfully hunted alone, the coyote will drift away from its compatriots when on the prowl for a meal. As a result,

173

during the early autumn, after the pups of the spring have become self-sufficient, coyote families tend to dissolve. Although the two adults may occasionally travel together, the majority of their hunting time is spent alone.

In more agricultural areas, the coyote forages on the remnants of crops remaining in the field after the harvest. Also, in farm country it will stalk domestic poultry and other forms of livestock, as many rural landowners can colorfully relate.

In the central Adirondacks, however, there are few farm animals or associated vegetable matter which the coyote can eat during winter. Additionally, most of the small creatures of the forestlands are quick to scurry up the nearest tree at the first hint of danger, rather than running into the underbrush. This limited availability of small ground dwelling animals in the wilderness woods causes this resourceful animal to adopt a different method of acquiring food.

Rather than concentrating on small animals during winter, the Adirondack coyote focuses the majority of its attention on deer. Bringing down one of these agile hoofed mammals requires an entirely different hunting technique than that used for small game. Rather than hunting alone, the North Country coyote remains in a small pack loosely scattered over an area. In this way, there is a much greater chance of flushing a whitetail. Also, a deer on the run is much less likely to evade or outwit all of the members of a pack, compared to a lone attacker. Consequently, rather than the family disbanding, the two adults and maturing pups of the spring remain together throughout the winter. Additionally, some evidence suggests that a few of the yearlings stay with their parents well into the following summer, despite their parents' preoccupation with rearing a new litter of pups.

As a result, the Adirondack coyote has taken on a more social, or wolf-like, personality. When studying the feeding behavior of this highly adaptable creature, it quickly becomes evident that it is able to modify its hunting style to acquire food within whatever region it finds itself. In the Adirondacks, the white-tailed deer has become its main quarry for much of the year, and this opportunistic animal has developed the skills and savvy for preying on them.

It should be emphasized that although the coyote routinely kills deer, it does not have a serious impact on the population of this big game species. Although it does destroy a substantial number of deer each year, the actual percentage taken seldom exceeds the ability of the whitetail to reproduce and replenish itself.

An Accomplished Hunter - the Bobcat

Like the coyote, the bobcat also turns to the white-tailed deer in the Adirondacks as its principal winter food source. With the migration of most of the birds and the hibernation of rodents, it, too, is confronted with a severe shortage of small creatures upon which it can prey. Additionally, as snow begins to cover the ground, the mice, voles, and shrews that populate the forest floor are seldom visible as they carry out their daily routine.

Unlike the fox, which relies on its acute senses of hearing and smell to locate small mammals moving about under Nature's white blanket, the bobcat depends mostly on its keen sense of sight to detect prey. As a result, after the snow arrives, and the cold confines the smallest forest residents beneath the powdery covering, the bobcat experiences great difficulty in finding a meal.

In areas in which snowfall is limited, the bobcat successfully hunts small prey for most of the winter. Open landscapes are also more favorable to this visually dependent predator. But the dense wilderness woods limits visibility, especially when snow clings to every bough, branch, and twig. This makes it more difficult for the bobcat to scan the ground for signs of life. Additionally, as the number of forest clearings and open fields decreases, so does the population of small ground dwelling creatures.

Just as snow reduces the bobcat's chance for spotting a meal on land, ice prevents it from detecting and attacking muskrats, small beaver, and other aquatic creatures. Of the smaller forms of wildlife that remain active in winter, only the porcupine and varying hare are open to attack, and the former has a sufficient defense to foil most attempts on its life. With its preference for living in areas of very limited visibility, its protective coloration, and its agility in the snow, the varying hare is also more than able to meet the bobcat's challenge. Therefore, as winter sets in, it is the whitetail that becomes its main quarry. While deer are less abundant in the Adirondacks than other types of wildlife, their larger size and dark gray coat make them easy to spot, especially against a snowy background.

Once it sights a deer, the bobcat stealthily closes in on it. Upon reaching striking range, this powerful mass of muscle, teeth, and claws then pounces on its unsuspecting prey. Despite its smaller size, with a weight averaging twenty-five pounds, it is capable of bringing down a whitetail in a matter of minutes. Although an adult buck or doe in its prime can sometimes break off an attack, other whitetails are seldom as fortunate.

Depending on its size, a deer can provide a bobcat with enough meat for two weeks or more. Since it is most successful in remaining undetected when it is alone, the bobcat rarely travels or hunts in a group. Families composed of an adult female and her litter of young typically dissolve in the late autumn, if not sooner.

The scarcity of deer in the Adirondacks causes the bobcat to travel far and wide in search of food. This is the prime reason why this cat possesses such a large home range in the northern woods. In fact, the bobcat covers a greater amount of area in the Adirondacks than in any of the other regions in which it exists.

Like the coyote, the bobcat has adapted to the austere nature of the Adirondacks' winter landscape by relying on the region's most magnificent form of wildlife to get it through to the time when birds, chipmunks, woodchucks, frogs, and various other animals become commonplace again.

Life Under the Ice

Few places in the Adirondacks seem as lifeless as the lakes and ponds during the winter. While the shallow waters along the shore harbor a greater abundance and diversity of life during the warmer months than other ecological settings, by December the area appears deserted. The only visible sign that something alive still exists nearby is the occasional presence of fox and varying hare tracks meandering in and out of the clusters of shoreline brush. In sharp contrast to spring, the only sound that interrupts the winter silence is the wind blowing across the freshly fallen snow.

Yet, despite this desolate scene, these weedy bays and marshy coves still serve as home to an exceptionally rich concentration of life. Beneath the annual ice sheet forming over the pristine waterways lies an immense collection of organisms, most of them dormant in the dark, murky ooze that covers the bottom.

Turtles, for example, partially embed themselves in the muddy silt as they wait out the long season. Although they lack gills, both the snapping turtle and painted turtle can remain submerged from the time that the ice first forms until the water warms in the spring. Since they are cold-blooded, the metabolism of these hard-shelled reptiles is greatly reduced, which means that their body functions slow to a bare minimum. As a result, their demand for oxygen also drops to an exceptionally low level.

Additionally, turtles are capable of absorbing small amounts of dissolved oxygen from the water. This is done by continuously pulling water into a special sac near their tail, as well as filling their throat with it. Both of these body sections contain a thin membrane that absorbs dissolved oxygen into their blood stream. While providing only a very limited amount of precious oxygen, this process still meets the turtles' respiratory needs.

Most amphibians depend on a similar process to stay under the ice throughout the winter. Many of the salamanders and frogs that populate the wetlands spend this season in the muck at the bottom of lakes and ponds. Amphibians have a skin that permits the diffusion of very small quantities of oxygen into their body. Although this does not allow them to remain underwater for any length of time in summer, it is sufficient to keep them alive throughout the winter in their quiescent state.

Also burrowed into the soft silt of many lake and marsh bottoms are a wide array of invertebrates. Many bugs that seldom frequent the water in summer have a wintery aquatic stage in their life cycle. Even though the water is cold, its temperature is preferred by many lower forms of life over the northern climate's harsher atmospheric conditions.

Some species of dragonflies are a perfect example of this type of metamorphosis. During June and July, the adults concentrate their time in open fields and semi-wooded areas, often at a fair distance from the water. As the season draws to a close, they return to a suitable pond or marsh where they deposit their eggs. After hatching, the fierce-looking larvae settle down to a life among the debris that covers the bottom. There they will reside until the following spring, when weather conditions become more acceptable to them.

The richness of life below the surface is also ideal to the otter's predatory needs. This sleek member of the weasel family is well-known for traveling under the ice in search of dormant animals to eat. Like the muskrat, and occasionally the mink, it uses the frequent air pockets under the ice where dissolved oxygen eventually settles out from the water.

A host of other creatures find refuge under the ice in winter, as well. Thus, as you stand on a frozen bay this winter, be assured that there is an unseen world just below your feet filled with life, although most of it is currently dormant.

Insect Winter Hideaways

To the delight of nearly everyone, winter is a season devoid of insect activity. From autumn until spring, it is possible to stroll through wooded groves, open meadows, and along the shore of marshes, swamps, or bogs without being harassed by flies, wasps, or mosquitoes. Even so, evidence of an insect presence can still be noted throughout the winter.

Like many other forms of life, insects, and other invertebrates become dormant or greatly reduce their activity with the onset of colder weather. Many Adirondack bugs winter in the soil, burrowing beyond the frost line or passing into a state of torpor in hidden spots on the ground. Other bugs live beneath the layer of ice that forms over the numerous waterways. Still others spend this season in shelters above the snow. It is their presence that can be noted by the careful observer.

The location of a colony of carpenter ants, for example, can be exposed by the activity of the pileated woodpecker, which feeds heavily on such bugs in winter. Standing dead trees are the prime sites in which ants set up housekeeping. Unlike termites, carpenter ants do not eat wood. They only tunnel through it, using it as the location of their nest, just as the much smaller brown ants make their homes in the soil.

In fall, members of a single colony gather in one massive cluster, usually in a chamber deep within the soft, dried timber. There they are insulated against the cold, and their combined body heat helps them avoid freezing.

The pileated woodpecker is their chief natural enemy during this season, as it is able to home in on their retreat and efficiently chip and chisel into the wood to expose them. The start of a deep cavity, indicated by numerous small chunks of wood scattered on the snow around the base of a tree, is a sure sign of the presence of an ant colony.

Pieces of bark pecked off the trunk, or wood that has been chipped solely from the surface of the trunk, also indicates the presence of other dormant insects. Various species of wood boring beetles deposit their eggs in summer just under the bark or in the wood's outermost rings. There the eggs hatched larvae, or pupa, remain until they mature into adults the following year. Woodpecker activity on the surface indicates the wintertime presence of other bugs, especially beetles, in these trees.

Another group of insects that spends winter encased in plant tissue are those that form galls. Certain species of minute flies, midges, and wasps lay their eggs in the stems of goldenrod, or in the twigs of willows and aspens. After hatching, the larvae begin secreting chemicals that cause a noticeable thickening of the plant tissue in that immediate area. This resultant tumor-like growth does not interfere with the functions performed by the stems, nor does it harm the plant. It does, however, add to the stem's insulation, making it a more suitable place for the larvae to spend the winter. Such bulbous deformities on the stems of plants are fairly conspicuous if you take some time to look for them.

While you are out this winter you may wish to examine a cluster of dried goldenrod stalks standing up through the snow, or look at the twigs of a quaking aspen, to see if you can find a gall or two. You might also note how many trees are being pecked on by woodpeckers. In aging forests it is surprising how numerous these insect homes can be during winter. But their numbers are nowhere near as great as the bugs which they produce come spring.

The Balsam Fir Tree

With Christmas a week away, many families are getting ready to bring a piece of the Adirondack landscape into their homes. While a manger may be the most appropriate symbol of the upcoming holiday, an evergreen tree has become the most prominent decoration.

Topping the list of conifers cut down as Christmas trees is the balsam fir. Unlike other evergreens, balsam needles do not easily drop off the branches when it is brought indoors.

After being cut and placed in a warm room, all trees quickly lose their moisture to the dry indoor air. All evergreens, except for balsam, soon shed the foliage through which this loss occurs. Under outdoor conditions dry air is usually accompanied by exceedingly cold temperatures, keeping trees in a dormant state. The warmth inside, coupled with the fact that it has been severed from its root system, causes a conifer to behave like a deciduous tree in autumn, dropping its foliage in order to protect itself from dehydration.

The balsam fir occurs in two different forms. In the dense under-story of mature, northern woodlands, its branches are widely spaced, and its flattened, inch-long needles grow out only to the sides of its twigs. This results in the thin, spindly appearance necessary in places of limited sun-light. Only needles angled directly outwards to capture the limited amounts of sunlight filtering through the overhead canopy ever form on its thin twigs.

In open areas, however, the balsam develops many closely spaced branches, giving it a far fuller appearance. Its round-tipped needles are more tightly packed and encircle the twigs, much like the sharp-pointed needles of the spruces. Having its needles arranged in all directions allows the balsam, when in open spaces, to more easily capture sunlight.

The ability of balsam fir to grow in a variety of northern settings makes it more numerous than most of the other trees that grow in cold, sub-arctic areas. Its ability to out-compete other forms of evergreens for growing space results in its dominance in these northern regions. Consequently, along with being associated with the Christmas season, balsam fir is one of the symbols of the Great North Woods.

Because of its widespread occurrence throughout the north, animals in such regions depend on the balsam fir in one way or another for their survival. Grouse, red squirrels, mice, and voles all feed heavily on its tiny, numerous, and nutritious seeds. These are borne in short, stubby cones concentrated near the ends of its uppermost twigs. Unlike other conifers, balsam cones stand erect rather than drooping down from a twig.

The soft needles that are perfect for supporting fragile pieces of tinsel also serve as an important food source for numerous animals, especially moose. In winter, moose consume as much as forty pounds of balsam fir needles per day. Deer also use the needles for browse, although they have a much more difficult time digesting it, and therefore rely on it only after exhausting all of their other food sources.

The varying hare also nibbles on the needles, along with chewing on the balsam's buds. The porcupine is still another form of wildlife that depends upon balsam fir for food, gnawing not only its needles and buds, but also its bark. In summer, some songbirds use its boughs to nest and rear their young. (A Christmas tree in the Kalinowski house several years ago had an abandoned thrush nest located deep amongst its branches.)

A final fact about balsam fir that should be stressed is its exceptionally low kindling point. This makes balsam easier to catch on fire than any other type of tree. The small blisters of resin on its smooth bark also contain a combustible chemical. Once it catches on fire, it burns quickly and is next to impossible to extinguish. Please remember to be careful of fire when singing "O Tannenbaum" around the tree this season.

A Partridge in a Pear Tree

Along with swimming swans, laying geese, French hens, and turtle doves, much attention is given this time of year to the partridge, which may or may not be found in a pear tree. Also known as a grouse, this chicken-like game bird is a common denizen of the many woodland thickets and forest edges that occur throughout the Adirondacks.

Unlike nearly all other birds populating our continent, the partridge relies almost exclusively on tree buds for food during winter. With its tough bill, this northern bird is able to pull off the tapered tips of twigs, as well as many of the buds that develop along their sides. Since the fibrous twig bulges contain a fair amount of nutrients, they allow the partridge, along with other browsing creatures, to survive this season even when no other foodstuffs are available.

After being severed from the twig, the buds are immediately swallowed and stored in an elastic sac located at the base of the partridge's throat. Known as a crop, this pouch holds a substantial supply of food, enabling the partridge to quickly consume a sizeable quantity of material. It has to be careful as it forages, however, since perching in the bare branches of a deciduous tree exposes it to both small game hunters and to any goshawk or great horned owl that may be lurking nearby.

While the grouse will dine on the buds of most hardwood trees, there are specific species that are far more attractive to it and better suited to meet its nutritional needs. Topping their list in the wilderness regions of the Adirondacks are the bulbous swellings at the tip of poplar twigs. White birch and alder are also frequently browsed, as are cherry buds.

In farm lands and places where ornamental or fruit trees now grow wild, the partridge can occasionally be found perching in their branches and feeding on any edible parts. During early winter, apple trees are especially attractive to the grouse since their limbs still hold a few green leaves or frozen apples. Along with its buds, the pear tree also contains an assortment of food for the partridge during the final days of autumn and the first weeks of winter.

After having filled its crop, the grouse travels to a place of cover, such as a dense patch of young evergreens. There it sits and rests as the food it has eaten passes into its gizzard.

Present in nearly all plant eating birds, the gizzard is a tough, muscular organ that helps grind the food birds swallow. Because birds do not have teeth, it is in this sac that pulverization of the food occurs. Usually there is a small amount of sand or a few, tiny pebbles that scrape against the food, helping to break it apart as the gizzard squeezes and churns the mixture. Since the woody tissue the partridge eats in winter is difficult to physically tear down, a fair amount of grit is needed in the gizzard to aid in the process. Along with many other seed eaters residing in the Adirondacks during winter, the partridge often finds this grit by pecking at the sand placed on roadways following a snowfall or ice storm.

In the more remote sections of the Adirondacks, where sanded thoroughfares do not exist, the partridge and its singing relatives must seek out a spot of dirt uncovered with snow. A gravel depression beneath a partially uprooted tree, or a steep bank under a protective overhang, are typical places that usually remain free of nature's white blanket, providing a source of grit to these feathery winter residents.

Although the partridge nibbles on a wide assortment of foods throughout the day, it feeds most actively in the hour or two following sunrise, and just before sunset. In the late afternoon it is especially active, usually plucking every aspen bud within its reach. In this way the partridge attempts to stuff enough food into its crop to last it through the cold nights, which are now about twice as long as the days. As a result, don't be too surprised to see a plump, grayish-brown bird perched in a tree in your yard sometime around dusk. Probably, it will not be in a pear tree, and it is just as likely to be there on the twelfth day of Christmas as the first. Or on Ground Hog's Day, for that matter.

The Red Fox in Winter

At first glance it seems impossible that a red fox could survive an Adirondack winter, considering the severity of the weather and the limited amount of food available to such a small predator. Bitter cold and biting winds combine to make living conditions far from hospitable. Additionally, frequent periods of deep snow seriously impede the ability of any creature to effectively hunt the few remaining animals that remain active during this bleak season.

Both the chipmunk and jumping mouse, upon which the red fox preys throughout the summer, go into hibernation long before winter firmly settles. Grasshoppers, crickets, beetles, and other large insects are also no longer available for the red fox to eat. (Despite a common notion that it dines solely on vertebrate matter, this rusty-tan canine actually relies heavily on invertebrates for food during the warmer months of the year.)

Although often considered to be a strict carnivore, the red fox frequently dines on the fruits of many plants. In summer, berries are a staple item in its diet and in autumn it gulps down its fair share of the beechnuts that fall to the ground in the mature woodlands.

The varying hare, with its snowshoe-like feet, is thought by many people to possess an insurmountable advantage over the fox in winter. Mice and voles also are thought to be uncatchable when snow blankets the ground, as both of these rodents confine their daily routines to the nooks and crannies below the snow's surface. There they are not only protected from the intense cold of the air, but are also out of the view of forest predators, such as the fox. Although mice and voles come to the surface from time to time, they spend very little time in the open, as there is nothing except danger for them there.

Despite these and other problems, the red fox is still capable of eking out an existence in the snowbound wilderness. With its exceptionally keen sense of hearing, it is able to detect the squeaking noises emitted by small rodents as they move through the blanket of white fluff. Although snow is an excellent absorber of sound, this ever-alert predator can still pick up and

home in on the faint vocalizations made by these animals.

The red fox also uses its acute sense of smell to locate prey. Even a foot or two accumulation of snow does not prevent it from zeroing in on the odors given off by the nest of a nearby rodent. By pouncing on such spots the fox frequently traps its prey. In other cases, it digs down in the snow with uncanny accuracy to uncover its unsuspecting quarry.

Mice and voles are not the only animals that the red fox captures in winter. Like these small rodents, the grouse often seeks relief from the cold by burrowing into the snow, but the fox will detect it and sneak up on this robust bird to capture it before it can break out of its snow shelter and escape to the air.

Even though it is protectively camouflaged, a resting rabbit is not invisible to the fox's discerning eye. Spotting its target, the fox sneaks up behind it, jumping it before the hare has a chance to use its unmatched speed and agility in a snowbound world.

The red squirrel is another animal that this fox preys on in winter. Although arboreal, the red squirrel caches underground most of the cones it feeds on in winter. As a result, it makes frequent trips from its treetop nest to the surface of the snow and below. Should a fox sight a squirrel entering its subterranean storage chamber, it will quickly position itself for an attack when the squirrel makes its exit.

Researchers report that the red fox consumes nearly a tenth of its body weight in fresh meat each day during the winter in order to remain healthy. While this seems like an impossible amount of food for it to catch at a time when prey is scarce, the red fox usually has little problem in meeting its demands.

The Whitetail Sheds Its Antlers

A popular scene displayed on greeting cards and on advertisements at this season is a large, regal, antlered deer standing against a snowbound mountain landscape. However, although the landscape during the end of December is often covered with snow, deer during this time of year usually do not possess antlers. Many people think that bucks retain their bony racks year round and that these impressive structures continue to grow throughout the life of the animal. In reality, deer antlers fall off during the early winter and are replaced the following year by a new set that grows during spring and summer.

Like moose and elk, the whitetail use their antlers solely to battle rival males during autumn's brief mating season. At the end of the breeding season, the antlers are no longer needed, and within several weeks they are shed, detaching directly at their base where they connect with the skull. There a layer of cells holding firmly to the skull for most of the year weakens, dissolving their supports. This is similar to the layer of cells at the base of a leafstalk, which deteriorates in the early autumn, causing the leaf to drop off the twig. In deer this process is triggered by the rapid decline in the blood levels of testosterone, a hormone that regulates their mating urge. After the antler falls, the exposed area on the skull scabs over and is covered within a week with a layer of protective tissue and hair.

In general, the antlers of larger and older bucks are shed several weeks before those possessed by younger deer. Older bucks are on the go nearly all the time, in some cases searching both day and night for does. This causes a decline in their overall health, compared to that of younger males which are less active during the breeding period. By mid-December, most of the larger bucks in the Adirondacks are antler-less, with the exception of a few smaller and younger males that keep their antlers until after the first of the year.

Because of improved food conditions in southern New York State, deer are better able to a maintain their health during rutting season. Consequently, the deer of that region keep their antlers for several weeks longer after the rut ends.

Another factor determining how long a buck holds onto its antlers is the abundance of unbred does in the general area. Where there are many does and only a few bucks, a doe can remain unbred well past the usual end of the mating season. Does that have not yet mated emit a chemical odor indicating their state to the bucks nearby. This smell in the environment

keeps the level of testosterone high in the males, allowing them to retain their antlers. The limited amount of deer hunting that occurs in the Adirondacks, especially in remote wilderness areas, has contributed to a healthy balance between bucks and does so that nearly all the does are bred by early December.

Once it drops off, an antler is next to impossible to find. After hunting season, only one to two whitetails per square mile occur in the central Adirondacks. This means only two to four antlers are to be found in an area of 640 acres.

Although quickly covered with snow, fallen antlers are often located by the small creatures residing on the forest floor. Mice, voles, red squirrels, and even porcupines love to gnaw on antlers because of the nutrients they posses. By the time spring arrives, many antlers have been chewed to the point where they are no longer recognizable.

If you happen to see a deer standing next to the side of the road from now until early May, do not assume that it is a doe simply because it lacks an impressive rack on its head. During the winter, both females and males are antler-less, although they still retain their regal look.

Index

Tom Kalinowski is a consummate naturalist who has lived and explored the Adirondacks for over 25 years. A former columnist for the *Lake Placid News*, Tom teaches physics and a course he developed on field biology and ecology at Saranac Lake High School. His nature articles have appeared in a number of magazines, including *Adirondack Life, The Conservationist,* and *Fur, Fish and Game*.

When not teaching and writing, Tom enjoys piloting his Piper Arrow across the Adirondack skyline. Born in Patchogue, Long Island, he lives with his wife and daughter in Saranac Lake.

Sheri Amsel has been writing and illustrating books and magazine articles for 12 years. Her enduring interest in natural history and environmental science led to degrees in botany and zoology from University of Montana and a master's degree in anatomy and biomedical illustration from Colorado State University. Sheri works out of her home studio in the Adirondack Mountains where she lives with her husband and two sons.